CYBERLAW CANADA

CYBERLAW CANADA

Jeffrey M. Schelling

Self-Counsel Press
(*a division of*)
International Self-Counsel Press Ltd.
Canada   USA

Printed in Canada.

First edition: January 1998

Second edition: October 1999

Canadian Cataloguing in Publication Data

Schelling, Jeffrey M. (Jeffrey Martin), 1966-
    Cyberlaw Canada

(Self-counsel legal series)
ISBN 1-55180-268-6

1. Computers — Law and legislation — Canada. I. Title
II. Series.
KE452.C6S34 1999   343.7109'99   C99-910825-5
KF390.5.C6S34 1999

Self-Counsel Press
(a division of)
International Self-Counsel Press Ltd.

1481 Charlotte Road	1704 N. State Street
North Vancouver, BC V7J 1H1	Bellingham, WA 98225
Canada	USA

To my wife, Sandy.

NOTICE TO READERS

Laws are constantly changing. Every effort is made to keep this publication as current as possible. However, the author, the publisher, and the vendor of this book make no representation or warranties regarding the outcome or the use to which the information in this book is put and are not assuming any liability for any claims, losses, or damages arising out of the use of this book. The reader should not rely on the author or the publisher of this book for any professional advice. Please be sure that you have the most recent edition.

All efforts have been made to verify the accuracy of Web site addresses upon publication. However, since Web site addresses are constantly changing, there is a possibility that not every cited address will be accessible.

CONTENTS

INTRODUCTION

The term *cyberspace* was originally coined by a science fiction author named William Gibson in his novel *Neuromancer*. The term refers to a virtual world created by a computer system. Cyberspace is now a commonly used term for the entire world of electronic communications operating over computer networks. Although cyberspace is commonly used interchangeably with the term Internet, cyberspace encompasses much more than just the Internet. It includes the World Wide Web, the Internet, bulletin boards, and anything else that lies beyond your computer keyboard. Cyberlaw, then, is concerned with the regulation of activities in cyberspace.

The laws regulating the Internet and on-line communication will have a significant impact on our daily lives, and on our businesses. The Internet is the talk of the decade. Everyone wants to "surf the Net." Everyone also has his or her own conceptions and misconceptions about how the Internet will change our future.

Some people say the Internet will revolutionize our personal and professional lives. Through interactive technology, we will be able to customize the type of information we wish to receive on a daily basis. The Internet will also free us from the bonds of the workplace and will allow us to work in the comfort of our own homes. Others say the Internet is nothing more than a gigantic photocopier and that it is a vehicle that allows persons to carry on illegitimate businesses such as promotion of drugs or child pornography.

There is no doubt, however, that the Internet is more than just a passing phenomenon. The precise role it will play in our future depends to some extent on how the Internet will be regulated by the law.

WHO OWNS THE INTERNET?

No one person or company owns the Internet. To the contrary, the Internet is a massive network of independent computers. This network is constantly growing. There are, however, a number of organizations that have assumed responsibility for coordination and standardization of the vast resources of the Internet. Some of these organizations are:

- Canadian Internet Society

This is a non-profit and non-governmental organization dedicated to the promotion and coordination of Internet technologies and applications in Canada. The goal of this organization is to represent Canada in international discussion of Internet-related issues such as domain name management and encryption technology management. Both of these issues will be discussed more fully later on in the book.

- Internet Architecture Board

This organization oversees research and development into technological standards on the Internet. It works to develop standard protocols and procedures for on-line communication through its Internet Engineering Task Force.

- Canadian Association of Internet Providers (CAIP)

Internet service providers, in Canada, are represented by this organization. CAIP represents commercial providers of internet services and works to facilitate the global expression of Canadian culture and commerce both within Canada's borders and globally.

Consider the following questions: What can be done about someone who posts a hateful message about a particular minority group on a bulletin board service that is subsequently distributed to thousands of people? Can your employer monitor your e-mail messages at work? Who is responsible if someone downloads a computer virus onto your computer system and wipes out all your computer data? How can we safely and securely pay for services we order on-line? What should the punishment be for someone who posts sexually explicit messages to a bulletin board service? How can we make sure that our children do not have access to such material?

The law plays a direct role in providing answers to these questions. As an Internet user, it is essential you have an understanding of the basic principles of Internet law.

What is the difference between computer law and Internet law? Computer law has been around for decades and has typically involved all the legal issues surrounding computer hardware and software. For example, the acquisition of computer hardware, the protection of software programs from piracy, the licensing of computer programs and patent issues surrounding computer technology — these activities are all governed by computer law. For the most part, the computer lawyer's role was to draft agreements for commercial transactions involving computers — either hardware or software.

The world, however, is going on-line and computer law has evolved over the last two or three years to encompass the law of the Internet. Basically, Internet law can be defined as a branch of computer law but one that is highly diversified. Internet law certainly involves negotiating and drafting contracts, but it is also much more than that.

What are some of the issues of Internet law that we will look at in this book? One of the first will be the legal issues of doing business in cyberspace.

The notion of electronic communication through linked networks of computers has been around for quite a while. Until recently, however, Internet use was typically restricted to military and academic applications. The introduction of the World Wide Web and, more importantly, the powerful "search engines" which allow you to easily find information on the Web has changed all of that. The Internet has become a much more widely used tool and as more people are involved in more commercial applications on the Internet, more legal questions arise. Is it, for example, safe to use your credit card number to order goods from an "electronic mall" on the World Wide Web? Is an electronic contract — which may be unsigned — an enforceable one? How can you be sure your name and other personal information will be safeguarded after having done business with a company on the Web? We will examine these and other security questions in detail.

Copyright and protection of proprietary information is another area we will explore. Most countries have copyright laws, and there are also international laws and conventions protecting proprietary information, and original thoughts and ideas. The problem with these laws is that they were developed for a world that relied entirely on written communication. The mind-boggling collection of data on the Internet and its broad dissemination via this new medium has posed new and challenging dilemmas for the law of copyright and trademark. How much protection do you need for your domain name? Do you need permission to download images you find on other Web sites for use on your own? Later in this book you will find out how to protect your communications from misuse by another person, and also avoid getting into trouble when using someone else's information.

The Internet offers vast and unique opportunities for criminals ranging from computer hackers to people seeking to distribute pornography. Internet law, then, involves some limited criminal issues.

We will also look at the issues of privacy and confidentiality. With great advances in the development of information technology, more and more of our personal information is being stored on computers. Each year it becomes easier to envision a paperless society where virtually all information is stored in computer memory. With that prospect comes the threat of stealing or altering information.

Every time an individual uses a credit card, deposits money in a bank, orders a meal at a restaurant, or even makes a telephone call, a record is entered into a computer. We will discuss some of these issues as they relate to privacy on the Web and how to ensure your privacy is protected.

Another privacy issue relates to the exchange of information by electronic mail or e-mail. There are laws, such as provisions in the Criminal Code, which make it a criminal offense to tamper with computerized information. These provisions are relatively new and their effective application to prevent unauthorized access to computer information is still to be defined.

The purpose of this book is twofold. The first is to educate the reader as to the basic concepts and rules that make up the law of the Internet. It is important to remember, however, that new laws are constantly being passed and old laws revised to deal with new and emerging computer- and Internet-related issues. The rate of change in these laws is extremely rapid — in the last 24 months, the volume of legal-related information on the Internet has exploded. Your obligation as a user of computers and on-line services is to have a basic knowledge of the legal issues that may affect you and your business. This book is an excellent starting point for learning about the laws of cyberspace. It is not, however, an exhaustive legal textbook.

The second purpose of this book is to provide practical advice that, if followed, should help a reader avoid basic legal disputes in many situations. This book is not intended to transform a reader into an expert in Internet law, nor to replace the need for legal advice when necessary. In a complicated situation, a knowledgeable lawyer can be of invaluable assistance and can save you and your company both money and legal hassles. With the legal information presented in this book, you will have a solid base for dealing with straightforward legal matters and you will be able to recognize when a situation dictates that you should obtain professional legal advice.

1
ON-LINE LIABILITY

a. TORT LAW

Whether you are an Internet user or you provide a service or product on the Internet, understanding what your responsibilities on-line are involves a look at tort law — one of the most diversified branches of law. A tort is a wrongful act or omission. In law, torts are typically compensated for by some type of damages, usually monetary. For example, if you do something that harms someone else, your act can be considered a tort and you may be required to pay damages to the person harmed by your action.

In Canada, tort law is generally based on common law — law created by judgments. This means that as each individual case is decided by the courts, that case becomes a precedent which helps establish a new law or modify an existing law.

Tort law is often confused with criminal law. If someone assaults you, for example, he or she may be charged and convicted by the government under the Criminal Code. Under tort law however, you may also sue the person who assaulted you for various damages, such as the time you had to take off work, out-of-pocket medical expenses, punitive damages, and compensation for the pain and suffering you and your family members experienced as a result of the assault.

b. LIABILITY OF COMPUTER PROFESSIONALS

The type and extent of damage caused by failures in computer systems and the cost of making good those failures can be unlimited. There have been many well-publicized examples of computer malfunctions, including jumbled inventories, overpayments by automatic teller machines, and the mailing of correspondence to wrong addresses. One need only look at the predictions that have been made in connection with the year 2000 problem to understand that in today's electronically linked society computer failures have the potential to cause damage of massive proportions. The role of tort law in cyberspace is to determine who should pay damages for computer mistakes or malfunctions.

As a computer professional involved in the sale of computer hardware or software, the management of computer systems, or the customization of computer software, you must know what your obligations and responsibilities are. Conversely, as a purchaser of hardware or software, you must know what your remedies are if the product does not meet your expectations.

It seems reasonable to expect that there would be many cases associated with computer use because of the numerous risks and liabilities associated with computers. After all, computers play an increasingly significant role in our everyday lives. We use them to do on-line banking, communicate with others, keep our records, and build the products that we use, among many other things. In fact, there are surprisingly few decided cases on liability for defects and malfunctions in computer systems. This a relatively new area and the law is still developing.

One recent case involved an interesting situation. A software and hardware supplier claimed it could replace existing computer hardware that no longer had the capacity to meet a client's computing needs. The supplier's representations went so far as to promise that if its products did not work for the client, the supplier would purchase and install a competitor's product for that client.

When the replacement of the existing system turned out to be an abysmal failure, not only did the supplier refuse to install the competitor's system as promised, but the client had lost all confidence in the supplier's ability to do so anyway.

The court found the supplier responsible for the cost of installing a competitor's system. In addition, a substantial amount was awarded to the client for the cost of its employees' time spent trying to make the defective computer system work.

How can you reduce your exposure to potential risks and pitfalls? Other than generally being careful in your dealings with other parties, you can limit your liability in certain circumstances through the use of a contract. For example, by including a limitation of liability clause, warranty, or guarantee in your contracts with third parties, you can limit your exposure to problems.

Responsibility for computer viruses is a good example. To ensure that you are protected if the proprietary software — the software developed for a specific use for your company

— you purchase contains a computer virus, you may want to include a warranty in your contract with the software provider saying that the software developer "warrants that the software is free of computer viruses or other devices that might detrimentally affect the functioning of your computer system." If you buy software off the shelf, you have only the manufacturer's warranty, which may or may not explicitly deal with software viruses. Most provinces have sale-of-goods legislation that contains implied warranties for the sale of goods, including computer software. These implied warranties say that the product should be suitable for the purpose intended and, presumably, free of viruses.

COMPUTER VIRUSES

Viruses are programs that replicate themselves through their incorporation in a host computer's software programs. There are many types of viruses and new ones are being developed all the time. After being imported into a computer via an outside source, viruses typically sit quietly in a host computer system until a predetermined event, at which time they usually destroy data and freeze the system.

1. Negligence

Every person is required by law to take reasonable care to avoid harm to those who may foreseeably be affected by their conduct. This is known as the law of negligence. The principle is illustrated by the famous English case where a manufacturer of ginger beer was held responsible to a customer for a snail found in one of its bottles of ginger beer.

The same principle holds true for a computer bug or virus in a computer system. For example, you hire a computer programmer to write an accounting program for your business, and six months after the completion of the program, you discover a virus in it which damages your computer network. If you can establish that the virus got into your system because of the programmer's negligence, the programmer could be responsible for your out-of-pocket expenses and any other damages you can prove resulted from the virus.

There are thousands of cases that interpret the law of negligence; it is an area of law that is constantly evolving. Even a failure to warn of a risk may, in some instances, involve liability for negligence. It is, as a result, a good idea to label any diskettes or other media shipped to a customer "not guaranteed to be free of viruses."

(a) Preventive measures

A breach of this general duty of care may occur in the manufacture, design, marketing, installation, or any other activity related to the supply of computer goods or services. It can also occur through the ordering of goods and services over the Internet. How can you ensure that you are taking reasonable care in dealing with others on the Internet? There are preventive measures you can take to avoid getting into trouble in the first place:

(a) *Limitation of liability clauses.* If you wish to exclude or limit your contractual obligations and liabilities to potential customers, a good starting point is to include a limitation of liability clause in your contracts. If you intend to sell goods and services on-line, make it clear that you will not be responsible for damages that may result from the use of your product or service. Be as specific as possible. Will you be responsible for out-of-pocket expenses, loss of profits, and/ or lost data? You can limit your liability by including this type of clause in your contracts with your customers. Obviously this clause may not be a major concern if, for example, you are selling T-shirts on-line. However, if you intend to sell a software program or computer service, it is a good precaution to include this type of clause in your contracts.

Clauses excluding or limiting liability must be drafted carefully so they are clear and unambiguous. In addition, if you have drafted the clause, any uncertainty it might create will be held against you, particularly if you intend to limit your obligations.

A limitation clause must be brought to the attention of the other party to the contract or it may be considered not to form part of the contract. A simple way to ensure that this obligation is met is to have your client read the clause and initial it. The following is a sample limitation of liability clause:

> ABC Corporation will not be liable to XYZ nor to any other party for any loss, damage, claim, or expense of any kind caused directly or indirectly by the furnishing of information, equipment, and/or services pursuant to this contract. It is understood that ABC Corporation will also not be liable for any interruption of service, loss of business, destruction of data, or any other damage suffered by XYZ however caused.

Chapter 4 discusses contracts, specifically electronic contracts, in more detail.

(b) *Be careful what you say to your customers.* Your customers will remember what you say. In certain circumstances, you could be held responsible for a promise made to a customer. As a Web site developer, for example, you could be liable for damages to a customer if you make exaggerated promises about the performance of a Web page you had produced for a customer.

Consider the situation where you design a Web page for a customer that allows people to place orders on-line. Your relationship with the client sours when the Web page performs miserably. Users find it cumbersome to use and stay away from the product in droves. Could you as the Web site designer be found liable for the customer's lost business? Maybe. If your customer can prove that he or she relied on your specialized skills, knowledge, and claims to his or her detriment, you could be responsible for any resulting damages or loss of sales.

All too often, people overlook simple methods of ensuring that there is no confusion between them and their customers. For example, make sure that you and your employees keep notes of conversations with customers, particularly if you are giving them information on how a product will perform or how much it will cost. Then send a fax or e-mail confirming the details of your conversation or agreement.

Also, look closely at the claims that your promotional literature makes about you and your company. It is probably not a reasonable representation to boast 24-hour service on your Web site if you are a one- or two-person consulting company. The wording of any promotional literature that may be misleading will be used against you if a problem arises.

(c) *Know your customers.* Do a proper and objective evaluation of what your customer's needs actually are. For example, if a conservative accounting firm hires you to design a Web page, and the partners of the firm are extremely busy and not terribly concerned about having anything more that a simple presence on the Internet, the firm probably isn't interested in having a high-maintenance Web page with a lot of bells and whistles. Simplicity and professionalism are the keys to good relations with this type of customer.

Ask yourself, do you and your employees have the skills necessary to meet the customer's needs? Have you worked with their particular applications in the past? You will find that your relationship with your customer will sour unless both parties' objectives are reasonable from the start. Taking on more than you can handle could lead to downtime, glitches, lost data, missed deadlines, and other problems for which you may be held responsible.

(b) Have you been negligent?

If you are not sure whether you have, in a particular situation, been negligent, ask yourself these questions:

- Was information given on a subject in a situation where someone relied on your expertise or specialized knowledge?

- Was there a duty owed to the person who relied on your advice? For example, you will not likely be held liable for a statement you made in passing at a cocktail party. On the other hand, if someone is paying for your specialized services as a software expert, it is quite reasonable that you would owe a duty of care to that person.

- Is it reasonably foreseeable that a person might be affected by your conduct? The foreseeability factor may be express or implied. In other words, it would probably not be a good defence to suggest that an accounting firm would not be adversely affected by your having corrupted its client database. The risk of harm is implied in your dealings with a company that relies heavily on its computer system.

If the answer to any or all of the above questions is yes, you must exercise care and bear in mind the obligations that the law of negligence imposes on you.

2.   Misrepresentations

Under common law, you may also be held responsible for damages from misrepresentations made negligently, fraudulently, or recklessly. There is a difference between a reckless or negligent misrepresentation and one that is outright fraudulent.

Take, for example, the phrase, "This software program is compatible with Windows 3.1." This claim may be reckless or negligent if it turns out that the statement was made out of ignorance and without the claimant having ascertained that the software is compatible with Windows 3.1. However, the statement is fraudulent if the claimant knows when making the claim that the software is not compatible with Windows 3.1.

Sometimes fraudulent misrepresentations can lead to charges of fraud. Fraud is, however, difficult to prove since it requires proof that there was an *intention* to defraud at the time the statement was made.

False advertising is closely related to the notion of misrepresentation. Unrealistic or exaggerated claims in promotional materials could form the basis of liability in tort. In addition to common law, most provinces also have consumer protection legislation, such as the Business Practices Act in Ontario, which prohibits advertising likely to mislead or deceive.

3.   Liability for professional advice on the Internet

In the last several years, a number of professional firms and companies offering professional advice have sought not only to establish themselves on the Internet, but to go one step further and offer customized professional advice on the Internet for a fee. For example, accounting firms offering financial advice and lawyers offering customized legal advice. This can be problematic and should only be contemplated with extreme caution.

First, though, a word about generic professional advice on the Internet. From the perspective of the person offering the advice, make sure there is no doubt that the advice is generic in nature and not to be relied upon in specific circumstances. After all, every profession has "gray areas," and what might be a good idea with regard to one set of facts might not apply in another. This objective can be accomplished through the use of a clearly worded and prominently displayed disclaimer. From the viewpoint of the recipient of generic professional advice from the Internet, be aware that no situation is the same and accordingly, if in doubt, get advice from a professional the old-fashioned way — in a face-to-face meeting.

Now back to the offering of customized professional advice on the Internet. In short, the law will not likely make any distinction between advice offered on-line or otherwise. The giver of such advice will be responsible and potentially liable regardless. Such advice, then, must be given in a manner that complies with applicable professional codes of conduct and laws. Take the example of a recent English case. In this case, a company called Market Wizard Systems sold a computer program that recommended buy, sell, or hold options on selected stocks. The authors of the program didn't register the business under a UK statute which required registration for companies or individuals giving investment advice. The result? The court found the business to be unauthorized and illegal.

4. Vicarious liability

Vicarious liability is a common law rule that makes third parties liable for the actions of others. An employer could be held liable for the negligent actions of an employee even though the employer had not been an active participant in the negligence. The essential element for vicarious liability is the right and ability to supervise the activities of another. If, for example, an employee makes a negligent misrepresentation to a customer that causes damage to that customer, then the employer would be liable for such damage under the rule of vicarious liability.

For example, a radio station could be found liable for copyright infringement if one of its disc jockeys decided to play pirated music. The same holds true in the on-line world. It is quite easy to imagine a situation where an employer could be held accountable for an employee's defamatory e-mail message or a breach of copyright. How can employers protect themselves? Although it's not possible to avoid the rule of vicarious liability all together, employers can protect themselves to some extent by preparing clear policies for Internet use in the workplace and disseminating them in the workplace. These policies will be discussed later on in the book. Many employers also protect themselves from the negligent actions of employees through professional liability insurance.

5. Remedies and damages

If you are the victim of a computer-related negligence or misrepresentation, you should first give the person you are dealing with a opportunity to remedy the situation by repairing your equipment or software. Your main priority is, of course, to return your system to good working order as quickly as possible. Running off to court will likely only cause delays and frustrations as law suits typically take years to resolve, not to mention a great deal of money. You will, in almost all cases, be much better off reaching a cooperative compromise than pursuing what could easily turn out to be a lengthy court battle.

The first step is to decide what it is you actually want. What is the minimum compensation you will accept? Do you want your money back? Do you want the software or hardware replaced? Do you want your problem fixed by a different consultant? Is it necessary to maintain a relationship with your present consultant?

The next step is to read your original contract (you should have a written agreement). The contract may outline certain procedures for dealing with your complaint. For example, you may be required by contract to raise your complaint and try mediation before any court proceedings can begin.

(a) *Alternative dispute resolution.* Even if your contract does not require mediation, you may wish to consider it or other alternative dispute resolution (ADR) mechanisms for settling your dispute. Mediation is an ADR mechanism in which a mediator attempts to facilitate the resolution of a dispute. In the case of a computer-related problem, it is important to have someone with expertise in the subject area of the dispute as mediator. Mediation is generally nonbinding and is usually conducted at the mediator's or lawyer's office.

Arbitration, another ADR mechanism, might also be considered. Arbitration is also usually held in private, and can be binding or nonbinding, although it is usually binding. Parties to an arbitration can draft their own rules for the arbitration or can adopt rules governed by an arbitrations statute — most provinces have such a statute, for example, Ontario's Arbitrations Act. Like mediators, arbitrators are usually chosen for their credentials within the industry involved.

ADR is only an option if both parties agree to it. However, this is changing. There have been several test projects in Canada where arbitration has been incorporated into the court system, especially for commercial disputes. As well, courts are increasingly incorporating mediations into the rules governing court proceedings. One proposal is that parties must attend a formal mediation as a mandatory step before proceeding with a court action. If mediation or arbitration is a possible means of resolving your dispute, you may wish to contact a lawyer who specializes in the area.

ADR mechanisms have a number of advantages over court proceedings. Most important, from the perspective of a computer-related problem, is the ability to have someone with expertise in the subject area of the dispute attempt to resolve it. The parties to a mediation or arbitration also have the benefit of maintaining confidentiality and lower legal costs.

(b) *Court action.* If court proceedings are absolutely necessary, consider whether or not your dispute falls within the jurisdiction of the Small Claims Court. Most litigants in Small Claims Court are not represented by lawyers and the procedure is straightforward.

If all other avenues of settling your dispute fail, it may be necessary to go to court with the assistance of a lawyer. Again, you must ask yourself, what is it you really want?

Consider the remedies open to you:

(i) The basic principle is that our courts award damages to allow the injured party to recover what he or she has lost: to return the injured party to the same position he or she was in before the problem.

For example, a computer consultant provides you with a diskette that contains a virus that wipes out all your client records. If you are able to prove that the computer consultant neglected to check that the diskette did not contain viruses, a court is likely to compensate you for any necessary or reasonable time spent in rebuilding your customer database. Of course, your case is stronger if you had a warranty against viruses in your contract (see section **b.** above).

(ii) The court may also award damages for loss of profits as a result of your downtime, assuming you are able to properly quantify such loss. You should be aware, however, that the law is reluctant to award damages in negligence for purely economic losses, that is, those not associated with physical injury to your property. The reason is simple and stems from the notion of foreseeability. While it is foreseeable that someone would have to spend time inputting client records to rebuild a database, it may not be reasonably foreseeable that your company might lose a million dollar contract because of the loss of a database.

One final word of caution about court proceedings. Going to court is expensive. Even if you are awarded damages, you will still have to collect them.

If the company or person you are dealing with is judgment proof, meaning they have no money or assets that you can legally get to, proceeding further may be simply throwing good money after bad.

c. LIBEL AND THE INTERNET

1. Defamation

Libel is a kind of defamation, and defamation is a category of tort law. A defamatory statement is one that causes a member of the community to think less of a particular person. In short, it damages someone's reputation or "tends to lower a person in the estimation of right thinking members of the community." Libel is defamation by writing.

Slander, another kind of defamation, is harming someone's reputation by saying something about them. The important point to remember, for both libel and slander, is the element of damage to a person's reputation.

DEFAMATION: TO FLAME OR NOT TO FLAME

Flaming is sending someone a nasty message or a message in harsh tones, usually written in anger. Flames usually occur on on-line bulletin boards or in chat groups. Bulletin boards are meant to encourage free communication on a particular subject. Unfortunately, some people get carried away by making personal attacks in response to certain messages.

Defamation can occur on a computer system in a number of forms. E-mail can contain defamatory statements. Material posted on a bulletin board can be defamatory, as can material contained in electronic periodicals, file servers, and data-bases. Here are some actual examples of libel taken from actual cases:

(a) An archaeologist from the University of Western Australia won an award of A$28 000 in a suit filed against a colleague who made defamatory remarks about him on the Internet.

(b) A medical equipment company in New Jersey sued an investor whose critical remarks on the Prodigy Money Talk bulletin board allegedly caused the company's stock to tumble. The case was settled out of court.

As you can see, the laws of defamation present a number of risks and obligations to a computer user.

The law of libel has typically concerned itself with news-papers. Publishers of newspapers that publish stories which damage a person's reputation may be held liable for dam-ages. In a typical libel case, the newspaper, the publisher or editor, and the reporter who wrote the libellous story could all be possible defendants.

The same is true for on-line libel. People who post mate-rial to the Internet can be considered to occupy the journal-ist's role and may be found personally liable for defamatory statements. The author of the statement could also be held responsible for damages.

BULLETIN BOARD SERVICES

BBS is an abbreviation for *bulletin board service* or *bulletin board system.* A BBS allows users to post information for others to read. In addition, a bulletin board will also store information which can be retrieved by users. Most BBSs are restricted to a very specific topic.

There are literally thousands of electronic BBSs and information services on the Internet. BBSs are much like the classified and editorial sections of newspapers. They contain personal information and opinions. Anyone can participate in a real-time conversation with another person on the Internet through the use of a BBS. Similarly, and relatively inexpensively, anyone can purchase BBS software and start his or her own bulletin board, becoming an on-line information provider. Can the owner of a BBS can be held responsible for defamatory comments posted to his or her BBS?

The short answer is, it depends. If it can be shown that the owner of the BBS did not verify his or her sources or posted an article knowing it to be false or defamatory, he or she could be liable to the person whose reputation is damaged in the same way that a newspaper editor bears responsibility for articles appearing in his or her newspaper.

In some cases, whether or not an on-line information provider has knowledge of the defamatory material will be clear. Some BBSs are moderated, and the comments on those BBSs are reviewed and approved by an intermediary. Other bulletin boards, however, are essentially free for alls, allowing individuals to post comments at will. In the second instance, the on-line information provider could be liable for damages even if he or she did not make the defamatory comments himself or herself because a degree of control has been exercised over the material.

Similarly, an on-line service (a proprietary service that provides private services such as entertainment news, software archives, and bulletin boards to its members) could be liable for defamatory statements made by its customers, particularly where the service provider monitors the on-line traffic of its clients.

If customers receive only access time from the company, and the company does not monitor communications, the company probably won't be found responsible for defamatory statements made by its customers on the Internet.

If, however, the service reserves the right to monitor on-line activity and reserves the right to terminate a user's privileges for improper conduct, then that provider could possibly be found liable for defamatory statements made by its customers.

In a recent decision, a U.S. court ruled that an on-line service provider, Prodigy, could be held liable for libellous statements made by one of its customers because Prodigy exercised "sufficient control" over its service to "render it a publisher with the same responsibilities as a newspaper."

2.   What have the courts said?

The notion of making a defamatory statement about someone via electronic communication is in its infancy. Accordingly, it is unclear how the courts will deal with defamation in the virtual universe of computer programs and data. Inevitably cases will arise for the courts' attention in Canada. The soundest advice for someone making electronic communications is straightforward — proceed with caution.

First, bear in mind that you may not be able to ensure that the communication is directed to the person intended to receive it. For example, a nasty comment about one of your co-workers e-mailed to a fellow employee may be misdirected into your superior's hands or to the person about whom the comment is made. This is true of all e-mail, whether it is sent over the Internet or via a company's own network.

Second, the potential for large damage awards in libel cases is great, so beware. Until the case of *Hill* versus *Church of Scientology*, in which millions of dollars were awarded to a lawyer on the receiving end of a defamatory statement, libel awards were relatively modest in Canada. The award granted in the *Hill* case means that the potential for large awards for defamation is now significant. Of course, each case is unique and must be considered on its own merits.

HILL VERSUS *CHURCH OF SCIENTOLOGY*

This case was decided in 1994 by the Supreme Court of Canada. One lawyer made defamatory statements about another on the steps of a courthouse and, most importantly, in the presence of the media. The facts of this case were not unusual. The amount of money awarded to the plaintiff was more than one million dollars — which was unusual. The *Hill* case has opened the door for substantial libel awards in Canada.

3.   Determining if a statement is libellous

Ask yourself these questions when evaluating a statement's potential for libel:

(a) Is the statement derogatory?

If the statement, given its plain meaning, tends to portray someone as a bad person, untrustworthy, or having engaged in criminal conduct, it is probably libellous. Not all derogatory statements are libellous, but most libellous statements are derogatory.

(b) Is the statement a statement of fact?

If so, can the truth of the fact be easily proven by a reliable and independent source? If not, don't take on the risk of publishing it.

(c) To whom does the statement apply?

To a professional person, such as a lawyer or a doctor, reputation is everything. Such a person will generally respond strenuously to any statement about himself or herself that may be considered defamatory.

(d) Are any defences available?

In Canada, certain statements may be published with impunity even though they are defamatory. For example, statements made during a court proceeding are privileged — that is, not subject to charges of slander or libel. Fair and accurate reports of such proceedings are similarly privileged.

As well, if a person making a defamatory statement can show that it was a fair comment on a matter of public importance or that he or she was justified in making the statement, he or she will also have a defence.

4. Remedies

If a defamatory statement is made about you, it may not be necessary to go to court and incur the time and expense involved with court action. It may be that the person who made the defamatory statement is willing to offer an apology which will be satisfactory to you.

If you must proceed with a court action, however, you should consult a lawyer. Each of the provinces has statutes dealing with libel and slander, and there are strict requirements for giving notice of your court action and short limitation periods for actually proceeding with your action.

5. Anonymous e-mail and trolling

One simply has to enter the search term "anonymous re-mailer" into a Web browser to be inundated with Web sites offering e-mail anonymity. These sites permit authors of e-mail to redirect a message so as to make the recipient unaware of the identity of the sender. The potential problems with anonymous e-mail are painfully obvious. In many cases, anonymity is used as a means of transmitting hateful or discriminatory messages.

Trolling can be even more problematic. Trolling occurs when someone posts a message on the Internet and makes it appear as if the message came from someone else. American courts have already had the opportunity to review this issue in the context of on-line service provider liability. In the case of *Zeran* versus *America Online Incorporated*, an unknown Internet user had posted a series of messages, without Mr. Zeran's authority, on an AOL bulletin board. These messages tastelessly glorified the tragic Oklahoma City bombing. As a result of this anonymous prank, Mr. Zeran received numerous derogatory and threatening telephone calls. Mr. Zeran sued AOL arguing that AOL had failed to promptly remove the offensive postings. Although Mr. Zeran's lawsuit was unsuccessful against AOL, he most likely would have been successful in a defamation action against the author of the anonymous message, had he been able to determine his or her identity.

TIPS AND TRAPS

NETIQUETTE — AVOIDING DISPUTES ON THE INTERNET

Regardless of the medium involved, there are generally accepted rules of communication that must be followed by all individuals. Usually when you write a letter to someone, you follow accepted rules of conduct. For example, you would ensure that the person's address is on the letter, address that person as sir or madam, and you would sign the letter.

The same holds true for the Internet. The rules of netiquette are more or less a codification of good manners. It is not considered good manners to yell at people, and it is assumed that you should say thank you when someone does something for you.

People who do not know and abide by the rules of netiquette are easily recognized as newbies or newcomers to the Internet. Of course there is nothing wrong with being a newbie — everyone has to learn sometime. What you do want to avoid, however, is being seen as lacking good manners.

Here are some important points of netiquette to remember:

1. Watch your tone

It is very easy to communicate with e-mail. So easy, in fact, that many people sacrifice clarity of communication for brevity. What might sound reasonable in ordinary speech could be interpreted as aggressive, abrupt, or rude. Many businesspeople, although they would ordinarily spend the time to revise and properly draft a letter, regularly fire off an electronic mail message without thinking much about it. Always have a good look at your e-mail messages before sending them off.

2. Be polite

Do not be coarse, vulgar, or suggestive. These kinds of expressions are not acceptable in ordinary speech and are therefore not acceptable on the Internet. You should also be mindful of the fact that, especially in an employment context, people may be watching what you are writing in your e-mail messages. Messages you write today may come back to haunt you tomorrow.

3. Be discrete

Do not send any messages that you would not otherwise send in a letter. In other words, do not be deceived into thinking that someone other than the intended recipient will not be able to read your e-mail message. Messages can very easily be forwarded or misdirected.

4. Verify addresses

Double check the addresses of outgoing e-mail messages and ensure that your messages are properly addressed. It is very easy to imagine a difficult situation developing from an e-mail message redirected to the wrong person within a workplace, or among family and friends.

5. Be courteous to other users

If you inadvertently discover someone else's password, let them know. Under no circumstances should you use another person's account without his or her permission nor should you in any way compromise that person's digital security.

Similarly, if you discover a bug in a computer system, tell the system supervisor. Do not simply assume that it is someone else's responsibility. Most important, if you know or hear of someone attempting to break into another person's system, tell the system supervisor or the owner.

6. Don't flame

As indicated earlier in this chapter, flaming is considered very inappropriate on the Internet.

7. Don't shout

Shouting takes on a whole new meaning on the Internet. It involves sending someone a message in all uppercase letters. Many people think that sending a message in this fashion will encourage people to pay attention to them. Most often, precisely the opposite happens.

2
AN INTERNET SECURITY PRIMER

a. WHY DO WE NEED SECURITY IN CYBERSPACE?

Although there are many barriers to the widespread acceptance of electronic commerce, these barriers are quickly disappearing. First, the tremendous growth in Internet use has focused attention on a glaring concern about privacy on the Internet. Until recently, there have been very few safeguards to ensure that messages are not intercepted, read, or altered.

The recent growth surge of the Internet has also focused attention on the great potential for fraud and deception over the Internet, since transactions on the Internet are largely anonymous. People are merely blips on a computer screen.

For example, it is not easy to trust a faraway merchant whom you have never heard about or seen. The answer lies in improved security measures on the Internet.

b. HOW MUCH SECURITY DO YOU NEED?

If you have one computer, Internet security is a relatively simple matter. You can buy virus protection software to protect your data from outside threats and you are probably familiar enough with your computer from your regular use of it to become aware of any threats. You also can back up your data on a regular basis so that you are not severely threatened by the prospect of an invading Internet virus.

Internet security is, however, a much more serious topic for an organization that has more than one or two computers. While you may have some, if not all, of your data backed up, it can still be very costly and time consuming for all your data to be restored if there is a disaster. In addition, such a business will have serious concerns about outside unauthorized access to its confidential records.

You can easily imagine the technological challenges a business with 100 computers faces. At any given time, 100 employees may all be connecting to the Internet. That means there are 100 chances for one of those Internet users to allow an invader to penetrate your computer system and wreak havoc. This is where firewalls come in.

c. WHAT IS A FIREWALL?

A firewall allows you to manage your Internet traffic. It ensures that all traffic passes through a single point which effectively filters all data, retaining useful information and keeping attackers out.

Firewall is a generic term. You can buy software-only firewalls which, for example, you can configure to bar certain employees from accessing the Internet. You can also have a firewall constructed from both hardware and software components.

A typical firewall setup will use a router — a hardware device — to block certain protocols that hackers might use to break into your computer system. This router limits the kinds and sources of data traffic allowed onto your system, thereby making the hacker's job much more difficult.

Another way of setting up a firewall is to put a sacrificial computer on the outside of your firewall. This computer will run all your services that are accessible to outside traffic. Such sacrificial computers are sometimes called proxy servers. Proxy servers are on the outside of your network and allow you to access the Internet either indirectly or directly. The proxy server protects against unauthorized access because it is the only element of your system directly exposed to the outside world.

Not everyone needs to go to the expense and trouble of setting up a firewall. If your business has only one computer with Internet access through a modem, a firewall may be more than you need. You can also get by without a firewall in the following situations:

- If you do not store any confidential customer information, credit card numbers, or any other confidential data on the computers used to connect to the Internet.

- If your only use of the Internet is for e-mail and you use a specialized mail server that dials up your access provider, exchanges messages, and then hangs up, it is unlikely you will need to set up a firewall as your connection time will be quite limited.

It is important to note that firewalls protect against unauthorized access and are of limited use against viruses. You must also still be aware of who is accessing your data internally. Unfortunately, one of the biggest threats to your confidential data is an internal leak.

MORE INFORMATION ON FIREWALLS

Check out these Web sites for more information:

- www.soscorp.com

This is a Web page produced by S.O.S. Corporation, a New York City–based company that produces an Internet security application called Brimstone. You will also be able to access other information from its home page, including a document titled "Introduction to Firewalls."

- www.digex.net/showcase/papers/security-1.html

This site is a one-stop source for Internet security measures and products.

- www.first.org

This is a Web page maintained by the National Institute of Standards and Technology in Gaithersburg, Maryland. The Web page is billed as a computer security resource clearing house.

d. ENCRYPTION

Encryption transforms your data into an unreadable mass of letters and numbers. This mass of letters and numbers can be easily translated into a readable form but only by the person who has a key to decrypt the information. The purpose of encryption is to maintain security of transactions on the

Internet. Encryption technology is of great interest to organizations doing business on the Web because it assures the privacy of highly sensitive transactions. Banking is a good example. Most forms of on-line banking use encryption that protects against outside invasion.

The Internet is an open system: messages are exposed while in transit to another person on the Internet. Using encryption, you can scramble sensitive files such as your password file to make them more difficult for someone to use without your permission. If encryption technology were not available, many forms of on-line commercial activity would not be pursued.

1.   How does encryption work?

Encryption is much like a secret code and the way it works is quite simple. Encryption software uses a complex mathematical equation to translate the material you are sending over the Internet into scrambled text called ciphertext. The ciphertext is impossible to read. It can be translated and read only by someone who has a key to the translation. Fortunately, you don't have to be a math professor to use encryption software; the crucial formulas that these programs use are incorporated into user-friendly software programs.

Here are some examples of encryption software:

- *Pretty Good Privacy (PGP)* is a very secure software program that is widely used in both Canada and the United States. Businesses tend to choose PGP because it is very hard to crack.

   Governments do not like it for the same reason. It is, as a result, illegal to export from the United States (the United States has classified it as a weapon because it could be used to cipher top secret information). Although PGP is widely used in Canada, versions of the product are available at sites outside the

United States, thus making U.S. export laws irrelevant. For more information about PGP, see www.pgp.com.

- *Clipper.* Clipper is a widely used encryption system which makes use of an encryption scheme called Skipjack. The downside with Clipper is that you must purchase a computer chip to make it work.

- *Secure Sockets Layer* (SSL). This is encryption software developed by a company which is well known for its Web site browsing tools — Netscape. You can check out a demo of this security program at home11. netscape.com/assist/security/ss.

- *DES* (Data Encryption Standard). DES was invented by IBM in the 1970s and adopted as the U.S. government standard. It is not 100% foolproof. While it is perfectly adequate for most users, it has been demonstrated that a large corporation or government (in other words, someone with virtually unlimited resources) could decipher a DES encrypted message. Because of its age, DES is used less often today than in the past.

2.   Private versus public key encryption

In private or conventional key cryptography, a single key is used to encrypt and decrypt a message. Both the sender and recipient of the message must have a copy of the same key and both the sender and recipient must make sure that the key is kept secret. This conventional cryptography is quick and easy, but it may not be useful when, for example, one sender is sending a message to 1 000 recipients. This is where public key encryption becomes useful.

In public key cryptography, also known as asymmetric cryptography, a pair of complementary keys are used. One key is shared and the other is kept private. The person who holds the private key (usually the sender) is the one who has the sole responsibility to keep that key secure and completely private. The public key can be widely disclosed without a break in security.

Public key encryption has permitted and will continue to permit the phenomenal growth of commercial activity on the Internet. In fact, public encryption technology is the basis for creating digital signatures. Digital signatures will likely form the basis for establishing secure on-line transactions in the future.

There are currently no legal restrictions prohibiting the use of encryption technology in either Canada or the United States. Governments are, however, cautious about encryption. Good encryption technology allows completely private communication. This means that communications by people wanting to avoid paying tax, those wanting to deal in sensitive government information, or those wanting to conduct illegal activities can potentially be conducted privately over the Internet. Encryption permits anonymous and secret communications safely outside the government's scrutiny. Imagine the possibilities.

Some countries, such as Spain, have made encryption illegal. Other countries have placed restrictive controls on encryption technology. The government of France, for example, requires a copy of your key and also requires that an encryption user obtain a government permit. If you are involved in a large international commercial venture using encryption technology, you should get legal advice.

Despite its obvious strong points, it would be a mistake to think that cryptography is infallible. It is not. There will always be someone with the time, computing resources, and incentive to challenge new encryption technology. For example, in the fall of 1995, a French college student cracked a commercial transaction encrypted with Netscape browser software. The procedure took him eight days and he had to use 120 workstations simultaneously in order to do it.

Encryption technology is changing rapidly as it must keep ahead of hackers who are continuously trying to decipher encrypted messages. You must, therefore, keep current with new encryption technology.

TIPS AND TRAPS

SELECTING GOOD PASSWORDS

Computer thieves can use high-tech tools that let them break into corporate information systems. For example, thieves or hackers can use programs that try every possible combination of letters, numbers, and punctuation in order to break your password. This is in addition to the less sophisticated approach of making a number of educated guesses about what kind of password you have selected.

Hackers, though, tend to take the path of least resistance. Your best protection is to choose a password that will make it very difficult for a hacker to figure out. Here are some general guidelines to consider:

What not to use:

- Do not use a password shorter than five characters. Some programs will not even accept a password of less than four or five characters.

- Do not use your first or last name in any form, e.g., spelled reverse or in short form. You should also stay away from names of immediate family members such as spouses, children, or pets. These would be the first passwords a disgruntled co-worker will use in attempting to decipher your password.

- Do not use other information easily obtained about you such as birth dates, phone numbers, licence plate numbers, and addresses.

- Do not use a password of all digits, such as 99999, or all of the same letter.

What you should use:

- Use a password with a mix of upper- and lower-case characters. Throw in some non-alphabetic characters for good measure such as digits or punctuation.

- Use a password that is easy to remember, while bearing in mind that it shouldn't be too easy for someone else to figure out. Obviously, your password is of no use to you if you forget it.

- Use a password you can type quickly. If you are able to enter it quickly, it is harder for someone to steal your password by watching you enter it.

- Do not keep your password written down where it could easily be seen by others. Do not share your password with a co-worker.

3

BUYING AND SELLING GOODS ON-LINE

The development of electronic cash and payment mechanisms as substitutes for traditional cash transactions is one of the main reasons for the tremendous growth in interest in the Internet over the last several years. Businesses of all types can now use the Internet to conduct electronic commercial transactions anywhere in the world. Today, retailers are selling everything from computer hardware to T-shirts on-line. All the major Canadian banks offer on-line banking, and many financial institutions now accept credit card applications via the Internet.

A number of key issues relate to electronic commerce. For example, how does an on-line vendor create and enforce an on-line contract?

Outside the cyberworld, most contractual relations are entered into when two or more people agree to and sign a contract. Signing an electronic contract is clearly not possible. Questions therefore arise: Does the law require that a contract be signed for it to be enforceable? How can an electronic contract be signed? We will look at the nature of contracts and the issues surrounding them in chapter 4. In this chapter, we will examine how money moves around in cyberspace.

E-COMMERCE

E-commerce is a general term that applies to all commercial transactions using electronic means. Open networks like the Internet, closed networks such as Electronic Data exchanges (EDI), and customized and controlled networks (Intranets) all come under the label of e-commerce.

a. ENSURING ELECTRONIC PAYMENT SECURITY

1. Using your credit card on the Internet

Obviously actual bills and coins cannot be exchanged in cyberspace, but these days, most of us do not use cash anyway. Instead, we rely on cheques, credit cards, and most recently, debit cards. Many of our purchases and payments, such as mortgages, RRSPs, and utility payments, are automatically debited from our bank accounts. What about purchases made over the Internet? How can one safely and securely pay for items bought on-line? Is it safe to use credit cards for on-line purchases? There are now mechanisms available to help ensure the security of on-line payments.

Goods or services obtained on-line can almost always be paid for by credit cards. The process is no different than ordering goods by mail or over the telephone. There are, however, problems associated with using credit cards for on-line purchases. The first and most obvious is that someone may intercept the credit card number and use it to purchase goods without the card holder's knowledge or consent.

Most of us have heard horror stories related to Internet credit card security. There is no question that it is sometimes possible to steal a credit card number over the Internet. In reality, however, giving a credit card number over the Internet is probably no more of a security threat than any other credit card transaction. It is possible that a determined hacker might create a program to retrieve credit card numbers from the general flow of information over the Internet, but it is just as likely that anyone that you give your credit card to, whether in person or over the telephone, may use it wrongfully.

Still, if you have a Web site and want to be able to accept credit card payments, you will have to address the widespread perception that credit card use on the Internet is dangerous in order to alleviate the fears of potential customers.

(a) Encryption

One way to safeguard credit card transactions is to use public key cryptography. Cryptography is the use of software programs to scramble messages on the Internet to avoid the interception of private or business-related communications. Public key cryptography scrambles numbers (such as credit card numbers) and other personal or corporate data before it is sent over the Internet and then enables the receiver to unscramble the message at the receiving end. Your Web site developer should be able to assist you in implementing this type of technology into your Web site.

Using encryption for an Internet sale assures a vendor of several things. First, that the order has reached the vendor without being altered or modified along the way. Second, that even if the credit card number and customer information being sent to you is being copied along the way, it will be useless because it is encrypted. Third, because the credit card number is encrypted, you have some level of assurance that it was sent to you by the person who claims to have sent it. Also, the sender must have the proper software to encrypt the credit card number, and usually only people concerned about security would bother to encrypt in the first place.

As the vendor, you will need a secure way to receive decryption keys from your customers. These keys allow you to descramble the encrypted communications you receive. Your Web site developer can help you set up the necessary technology needed for this type of system. Chapter 2 discusses encryption in more detail.

The cost of encryption measures varies, depending on your project. If your Web site cannot support encryption technology, it is a good idea to let visitors to your Web site know there may be a risk to them in delivering confidential information to you.

2. Digital cash

Recently there has been a great deal of publicity about digital or electronic cash. An electronic cash system is much more than a system for billing to a credit card, with or without the use of encryption technology. The simplest way of thinking of this virtual cash is as an electronic token.

There are two types of digital cash systems. The first involves a third-party intermediary between the purchaser and the vendor. This intermediary usually maintains an electronic account for the consumer and provides an audit trail to ensure security of purchases. A number of these types of electronic cash payment schemes are available for use over the Internet. Some of the more notable ones include:

(i) *TelPay.* TelPay is a Canadian service that allows you to pay monthly bills on-line. It offers special security features which guarantee confidentiality. One way that TelPay addresses consumers' fears about security is by ensuring that any unauthorized debits by TelPay to the user's account become TelPay's responsibility. You can find out more information about TelPay at their Web site located at www.telpay.ca.

(ii) *Digicash.* Digicash, a U.S.–based service, offers a secure way to buy and sell electronic coupons. Digicash is designed to be very similar to traditional paper and coin transactions. The transactions are completed using e-cash (electronic cash). Digicash supplies customers with software free of charge, and customers pay for purchases with electronic coupons from the Digicash bank.

The disadvantage of Digicash is that transactions can take place only between two users who are connected to a Digicash server which can convert e-cash into regular money and vice versa. For more information, visit the Digicash Web site at www.digicash.com.

(iii) *CyberCash.* CyberCash, also a U.S.–based service, allows purchasers to set aside money in a special digital purse. Funds are then transferred from the purchaser's digital purse to the vendor when purchases are made. Like Visa and MasterCard, CyberCash receives a fee for each transaction. The Cyber-Cash Web site is at www.cybercash.com.

The second type of digital cash system is based on the stored value card, or smart card. Smart cards are different from ordinary credit cards in that they have a microcomputer chip embedded in them. The chip stores electronic information and also controls who uses that information.

There are a number of players in the smart card market. The leader is the Mondex electronic cash smart card developed by the National Westminster Bank in England. The technology employed in the Mondex card stores money as electronic information. A Mondex card is unlike a debit card or a credit card because it can be used to transfer cash over the telephone and has a locking feature so that it can't be used if it is stolen or lost. Most importantly, because the Mondex card is the equivalent of cash, there are no carrying charges.

Smart cards have caught on well in Europe and are presently in wide use throughout a number of European countries. Smart cards are not yet, however, in widespread use in North America although they are gaining a toehold in some areas. Mondex, for example, recently completed a pilot project in implementing the use of Mondex cards with a number of vendors and consumers in the City of Guelph, Ontario.

b.   DOING BUSINESS ON THE INTERNET

1.   As a vendor

Most on-line purchases are made in the same way. First, the purchaser finds the virtual store, which may have its own independent Web site or may be part of a virtual mall including a number of stores. The purchaser is usually encouraged to browse the site to see what is available. Once the purchaser has made a selection, he or she is led, as part of the ordering process, through a series of screens containing contract terms.

There are a number of things you as a vendor can do to increase the probability that your contract is enforceable and to reduce the risk of the goods being returned.

(a) Implement software safeguards into your Web site to prevent a user from registering an order using gibberish. For example, the purchaser can be asked to select from a pre-defined list of responses, so that the prospect of someone entering gibberish is eliminated. Or, you could set maximum and minimum ranges for responses. If, for example, the purchaser enters more than six digits for a postal code, the entry will be rejected. These safeguards can be built into your Web page very inexpensively using the tools available in HTML, the program language commonly used to create Web pages.

A Web site developer can also help you develop an ordering process that uses protocols that ensure legitimate information is registered before a deal is closed.

(b) Set up your Web site so that the user is required to go through the contract registration screens before being allowed to go window shopping. The advantage of doing so is that the potential purchaser becomes committed to the site after having given personal information. Some visitors, however, may be put off by having to release personal information before seeing the goods.

(c) Provide the user with the option of leaving the contract screen sequence at any point in order to allow a doubtful purchaser to withdraw from the deal before it is closed.

(d) Require the purchaser to indicate consent to the contract terms in a positive and clear way. For example, have the user click on a designated box indicating acceptance of the terms of your contract, or type in his or her name into a statement such as: "I,_____, accept the contract terms of XYZ Company."

INTERNET ACCESS AGREEMENTS

Most people access the Internet through an Internet service provider (ISP). An ISP is a company that maintains a host computer (connected to the Internet) and which sells Internet access time, usually on a fee-per-hour basis. In addition, most access providers also sell value-added services such as Web page design and hosting. Most ISPs are local services, although many national firms (e.g., Bell Canada and Rogers Cable) have now realized the vast potential of the market for on-line services.

A number of contractual issues are involved with agreements between ISPs and customers. An ISP will typically want to prohibit users' unlawful conduct; for example, to prevent users from using the service to distribute pornography or for some other use that violates provincial or federal laws. The ISP may also want the right to monitor all communications through its service, as well as the right to terminate a user's rights if, at any time, the user has violated any laws.

Users, of course, want as much access time as possible for the least amount of money. Be wary of unrealistic promises. If an ISP is offering service at an unbelievable connection rate and price, chances are you will experience slow response time and perhaps even times when the Internet host computer is down altogether.

2.   The legalities of linking

In the early days of e-commerce it was generally accepted practice for the owner of a Web site to informally provide a link to one or more Web sites as a service to visitors of the Web site. For example, visitors to a Web site selling sporting goods would be able to take advantage of these links to visit other sites of interest such as sporting team franchises, sporting associations, and perhaps sporting goods manufacturers. As a result of the development of the commercial aspects of the Internet, this informal process has changed. It is no longer acceptable to link to another Web page without first obtaining the Web page owner's permission. This permission can be obtained via e-mail, but regardless, should be obtained in writing.

Why the need to obtain formal permission to link to someone's Web site? Simply put, it is a matter of being able to control how a product or service is marketed on the Web. Consider this obvious example. You have written a computer game and want to make it available for distribution. Clearly, you would not want your product associated with a disreputable person or company that wants to offer a link to your site on its Web page. This is a serious matter for companies that have invested vast resources in their reputation or unique trade name.

However, many companies use linking to their advantage in another respect. They allow other companies to link to their site as a means of generating revenue for their own company. If you intend to permit other people to market your product or service on their Web sites, then it is imperative that you have an agreement in place setting out each party's rights and responsibilities.

A sample Distributor Linking Agreement (Sample #1) follows. This agreement gives a basic idea of the type of matters that should be talked about between you and your distributor. For more complicated commercial situations, however, there is no substitute for good legal advice.

3.   E-commerce and the French language

The necessity of having a French version of information on your Web site is one of the most overlooked issues in the context of e-commerce in Canada. In Quebec, the Charter of the French language makes French the official language of government, business, and public communication. The charter has a number of implications for commerce on the World Wide Web in Canada. Simply put, the position of the Quebec government is that businesses employing 50 or more persons in Quebec have an obligation to offer French content to users of their Web site.

What if your business is located outside Quebec? In theory, the charter is of no effect outside Quebec, however, there are certain exceptions in which the Charter might apply. If there are factors that permit a real and substantial connection to be made between your e-commerce activities and the jurisdiction of the province of Quebec, then the charter might apply. For example, if your business is located outside Quebec but distributes products inside Quebec or employs persons in Quebec to sell or promote your product, then it would be wise to offer dual English and French content on your Web site. Take the case of *Investors Group Incorporated* versus *Hudson* as an example. In this case, the

Sample #1
ON-LINE DISTRIBUTOR LINKING AGREEMENT

THIS AGREEMENT is made between:

ABC COMPANY LIMITED ("ABC")

and

XYZ DISTRIBUTOR INCORPORATED ("XYZ")

IN CONSIDERATION of the mutual promises and undertakings in this Agreement, the parties agree as follows:

1. XYZ agrees to promote the ABC Web site by including a promotional link on XYZ's Web site provided such link is approved by ABC and provided XYZ's Web site is maintained at the same or higher level of quality as it existed on the date of this Agreement.

2. ABC grants to XYZ a non-exclusive, worldwide license to reproduce and publicly display ABC's trademarks and proprietary images on the XYZ Web site.

3. XYZ shall be paid a 15% commission on net revenues from the sale of ABC products less any returns from customers originating from the XYZ Web site. Upon approval by ABC, XYZ shall be issued a confidential account number which may be used to access ABC's distributor report page which will permit XYZ to track sales from its Web site.

4. Payment will be made within 30 days of the end of each calendar quarter. All payments will be made in Canadian dollars.

5. This Agreement shall continue in force for 12 months from the date it was signed by the parties. Either party may terminate this Agreement for any reason upon 30 days' written notice to the other. ABC may also terminate this Agreement immediately if the content or structure of XYZ's Web site changes materially.

6. XYZ agrees to defend, indemnify, and hold harmless ABC against any claims, actions, or demands resulting from a breach of the obligations in this Agreement.

7. Nothing in this Agreement shall be deemed to constitute either XYZ or ABC as agents, representatives, partners, employees, or joint

Sample #1 — Continued

venturers together for any purpose. Furthermore, neither party has
the authority to bind or incur liability on behalf of the other.

8. This Agreement shall be governed by the Laws of Ontario.

9. Neither party may sell, assign, or transfer their rights or obligations
    under this Agreement without the consent, in writing, of the other.

10. Neither party shall be liable to the other party for any incidental,
    consequential, special, or punitive damages of any kind whether
    or not such liability has been asserted on the basis of breach of
    contract or tort and whether or not either party has warned or been
    warned of the possibility of any such loss or damage.

Dated this _____ day of _____, 200-

_____   _____

ABC COMPANY LIMITED   XYZ DISTRIBUTOR LIMITED

Quebec Superior Court asserted jurisdiction over a defamation action even though the defamatory material was contained on two Web sites hosted on servers outside Quebec. The rationale here was that the court could assume jurisdiction because the parties were residents of Quebec and had business dealings within the province.

What are the consequences of non-compliance? A business with an establishment in Quebec that commits an offence under the charter may be subject to an inspection and inquiry by the Commission de protection de la lanque francaise on its own initiative or following the filing of a complaint. If the Commission finds that an offence has been committed under the charter, it will put the business on notice to remedy the breach within a prescribed time. In the event of continued noncompliance, penal proceeding will be instituted that may result in the imposition of fines. The situation is less straightforward for businesses with no establishment in Quebec. It is by no means settled whether an offence, for example, has been committed where a server is located outside Quebec but is consulted by Quebec residents.*

4. As a purchaser

What if you buy goods on-line and are not satisfied with your purchase once you receive it? Most provinces have legislation setting minimum standards for the sale of goods. This legislation provides that the goods you buy on-line must be usable for the purpose intended. Sale of goods laws also provide for an implied warranty of fitness. That is, whether or not the contract contains a warranty that the goods should be fit for the purposes intended, the law will read the contract between the parties as if such a warranty does exist. The implied warranty of fitness applies to goods only, not to services.

*The author gratefully acknowledges the permission of Isabelle Cantin, lawyer at the firm of Ogilvy, Renault, to use excerpts of her article titled, "E-commerce and the Charter of the French language."

A product's warranty should be valid no matter how you purchase the item, whether over the Internet or not. If you are not satisfied with your purchase, you should contact the vendor and request a refund.

Electronic contracts are discussed in more detail in chapter 4, but here are some further points of which Internet shoppers should be aware:

(a) Buying from a digitized picture or sample of a product. As with any photograph (and perhaps even more easily), computerized photographs of a product can be easily enhanced and, as is often the case, the actual product may not be as good in real life as it looked on the computer screen.

(b) Beware of unrealistic claims about a product. The Internet is worldwide: it will be extremely difficult, if not impossible, for you to remedy a unsatisfactory transaction with a company thousands of kilometres away.

(c) Be extremely wary of a Web site offering free goods or goods at a unbelievably low price in exchange for personal information, especially if it seems to you that the company is asking for too much or inappropriate information.

(d) It is highly likely that more and more standard transactions, for example, retrieving documents from an on-line news service, on the Web will be subject to a fee. As this becomes the case, don't lose sight of the fact that electronic money is money. Even though you may not realize it, the cost of all your transactions may pile up.

c. ELECTRONIC DATA INTERCHANGE (EDI)

1. What is electronic data interchange?

Electronic data interchange (EDI) refers to the exchange of routine business transactions on-line. Data is exchanged directly between computers using a standardized format so that the receiving computer can immediately use the data. More and more companies are using EDI to simplify procedures such as purchasing, scheduling, shipping, invoicing, and financial reporting. In fact, EDI is almost mandatory for any company that wants to enter into a business relationship with any of the large insurance companies or major department stores.

EDI transactions are typically set up between parties that have an ongoing business relationship and who wish to improve the efficiency of their commercial transactions. Without EDI, a complicated exchange of paper transactions in, for example, the form of orders, acknowledgments, bills, and remittances must be exchanged by the parties. Having computers do these transactions directly can reduce or eliminate the need for paper, and ordering delays can be reduced.

Consider this example: a large cruise ship has, of necessity, tens of thousands of spare parts which it keeps on board and uses as required. When a crew member uses a spare part, an order to replace the part is automatically placed with the supplier via EDI. The part is automatically supplied to the ship at the next port of call.

EDI is used in a wide variety of other business transactions, including the sale of goods and services, insurance claim processing, and income tax return filing: many people now file their income tax returns by e-filing them.

2. How do you set up EDI?

The complexities of setting up EDI are well beyond the scope of this book. It is not a matter of going to your local software store and buying an EDI kit for your computer. The parties must have compatible software and hardware, and EDI must work with every program in your company: your communications software, purchasing, and accounting among others. It must also be compatible with the systems of every company you do business with. However, technology is rapidly changing to make EDI easier and more affordable.

If you are interested in EDI, you may want to check out this site for a good explanation on how to get started: www.catalog.com/napmsv/edi.htm.

Electronic data interchange is usually done according to a master written agreement, or contract, often referred to as a trading partner agreement. This agreement outlines the rights of the parties doing business by EDI and should be negotiated with great care. Section **c.4.** below discusses some points you should watch for when negotiating such a contract.

3. Value added networks (VANs)

Company-to-company EDI is often conducted through one or more intermediary computer networks generically referred to as the value added networks (VANs). These are proprietary networks that are set up by the parties with the assistance of computer consultants. VANs provide a variety of services for EDI trading partners, such as translation services for EDI documents, system security, and certain record-keeping and audit functions.

A VAN will ensure that the parties use the same equipment and standards. Sometimes the VAN may facilitate the dealings between the parties by supplying a standard communications manual which acts as a guide for EDI communications. The most important aspect of selecting a VAN is reliability. If the VAN is supplying computing services, you will want to make sure there is as little downtime as possible.

4. Trading partner agreements

As we will discuss in the next chapter, a contract does not need to be in writing to be enforceable. A transaction conducted via EDI is technically not considered to be in writing; it is an exchange of information between two or more computers. However, the parties involved are usually able to produce computer printouts of each transaction. As well, these transactions are governed by a master contract, outlining the rights of each party. This master contract or trading partner agreement is written and binding.

The validity of EDI transactions has been recognized by most countries, including Canada and the United States, by an international treaty that eliminates the necessity of a written contract to create a binding agreement on the sale of goods.

Be sure to negotiate an ironclad trading partner agreement that will govern your rights and responsibilities before you embark on an EDI relationship. Here are some issues you will want to address when negotiating your trading partner agreement:

(a) *Security procedures.* What security is required for the transactions? Are the transactions highly confidential?

(b) *Fees.* What will the fees and charges be for the services that each party might require?

(c) *Technical standards.* What protocols and hardware are the parties expected to use?

(d) *Partial or garbled messages.* What happens if the transaction cannot be completed because of technical failure? Which party bears the loss in this case?

d.   ADVERTISING ON THE WEB: SPAMMERS BEWARE!

Until recently, commercial advertising was almost non-existent on the World Wide Web, mainly because the Internet was created and designed by computer technicians and academics. At its inception, the Internet was seen strictly as a vehicle for the free exchange of ideas. Advertising on the Internet was viewed as contradictory to the basic principles of the Internet and so prohibited. Things have changed dramatically.

Businesses and individuals throughout the world are discovering and exploring the Internet. Since the Internet is worldwide, businesses see the Internet as an opportunity to develop international business contacts. Many businesses are using the Internet as an information and communications tool for advertising, marketing, and customer relations. This new use of the Internet has become quite acceptable.

The notion for commercial advertising on the Internet has been taken to the extreme in the form of spamming. Spamming generally refers to the indiscriminate mass distribution of e-mail messages usually with a commercial intent. In a culture that has only recently accepted the notion of commercial advertising on the Internet, potential advertisers should be aware of the anti-commercial, anti-advertisement philosophy that continues to persist among many citizens of the Internet. Spammers, in particular, are not tolerated.

One of the most flagrant displays of spamming was committed by two lawyers. In April 1994, two Arizona lawyers, Siegel and Canter, posted an Internet advertisement to approximately 5 500 bulletin boards. Their e-mail message claimed that for a fee of $95 they would provide legal assistance to foreigners to enter the United States green card lottery. In reality, an application to enter this lottery can easily be completed without legal assistance and mailed to immigration authorities completely free of charge. What particularly enraged Internet users was that Siegel and Canter deliberately programmed their e-mailing software to send individual messages for each newsgroup. As a result, each bulletin board site on the Internet had to download the message many times instead of only once.

Siegel and Canter's advertisement drew angry responses from the recipients. Ultimately, the two were subjected to a massive campaign of harassment consisting of angry messages reacting to the ad and warnings from techies who threatened that they would write software that would roam the Internet looking for Siegel and Canter messages in order to delete them. The Siegel and Canter affair has cooled off but the message remains: be careful not to irritate the very people with whom you want to do business.

Direct marketing on the Internet, or spamming, is not illegal. For the most part, unsolicited e-mail advertisements are no different than junk mail you receive in your home mailbox. The difference is that as an on-line user, you are in a good position to stop unsolicited e-mail:

(a) Use a filter to delete messages from bulk mailers you have previously identified. For more information about filtering, check the Web page of Infinite Inc.'s Mail Filter and Robot Web page at www.ii.com/internet/robots.

(b) Send an e-mail back to the spammer along with your opinion of this kind of practice. If your company has an e-mail policy, tell the advertiser what that policy is and remind him or her that your employees may consider boycotting companies that advertise by e-mail spam.

(c) Call your Internet service provider. Most large ISPs have a customer service department that can be reached by e-mail. Send along a complete copy of the message and indicate your displeasure with it.

(d) Consider blacklisting the offending Internet advertiser. Several news groups on the Internet list some of the most extreme Internet abusers and also contain suggestions for appropriate Internet advertising.

U.S. LEGISLATION CONFRONTS SPAMMERS

Although Canadian legislators have yet to enact legislation dealing with spammers, many U.S. states have introduced laws aimed at eliminating spam and providing both service providers and aggrieved Internet users with a remedy. Pending U.S. federal legislation, for example, provides that any unsolicited commercial e-mail must contain a notice stating that the recipient will be removed from the mailing list by replying to the message with the word "remove" in the subject line.

e.   OTHER CONSIDERATIONS FOR ADVERTISING ON-LINE

Don't ever forget the Web is a worldwide marketplace. As a result, you really have no control over who will access your commercial Web site. Your Web site may be accessed in many different countries by many different people. This is the key aspect of the Web that is so obviously appealing to businesses that do business on the Internet. Laws, though, that govern advertising differ from one country to another. What may be legal in one country may be illegal in another. National television and radio announcers have addressed this problem by using disclaimers stating certain residents of certain states or provinces may not be eligible to participate or that the offer is void in certain areas. It may be necessary to use such a device in international advertising on-line — it depends on the nature of your product or service.

Special rules may also apply to goods or services that are marketed to children. Advertisers can even take common sense measures themselves to potentially reduce embarrassing or potential legal confrontations with authorities over the content of a Web site. Consider the following:

(a) Children should be reminded to ask their parent's permission before supplying personal information and should be told that supplying such information is only optional.

(b) The advertiser should disclose the purpose of requesting information and be careful to use language that a child can understand.

(c) If personal information is collected from a child, it is always preferable to obtain a parent's consent and, if possible, use a secure site for transmission of the child's e-mail address.

(d) If children are added to a mailing list, make sure a mechanism is available to a parent or guardian to remove the child from the mailing list.

TIPS AND TRAPS

LEGAL ISSUES AND YOUR WEB PAGE

The prospect of doing business on the World Wide Web has attracted all sorts of people and businesses. In most cases, an individual or company sets up their business on the Web by establishing a Web site. Virtually all forms of traditional commercial activity can be accomplished via a Web site, such as the sale of goods and services, advertising, and publishing.

Several legal issues must be considered regarding a Web site:

1. *Be careful when linking to other Web sites.* Most Web sites offer the Internet user the ability to link to other Web sites.

A link is simply the inclusion of another person's Internet address in your own Web site. Links are usually included in Web sites as a courtesy to the people who read the Web pages. For example, a Web page for a yacht broker may have links to other boating-related Web sites, such as magazines, marinas, yacht clubs, and weather services. Some Web pages may have hundreds of links to other Web pages, making them an excellent source of all different types of information on a particular topic.

Until recently, Web site designers have included links to all kinds of sites without obtaining the permission of the site owner. This practice has been challenged by a number of U.S. companies and the matter is being looked at by the U.S. courts. The U.S. court's decision may affect legislation in countries that have not yet dealt specifically with this issue, Canada included.

Although it is likely that a simple link is acceptable without obtaining permission, it is always better to get permission first. A simple request via e-mail will usually suffice. Chapter 5 discusses this issue in further detail.

2. *Do not misrepresent your product or service.* Provincial consumer protection laws set minimum business practices and standards for advertising of which you should be aware. In addition, be careful when linking to another site that you do not improperly suggest a relationship that does not exist with another company or suggest an endorsement by that company. For example, if a lawyer's Web page includes references to influential corporations as clients and then offers a link to General Motors, the reader might be falsely led to believe that General Motors is one of the law firm's clients.

3. *Be careful of infringing copyright.* Most Web pages use pre-existing content. For example, many graphics and images on the Internet are made available for

general use by people other than the creators. Make sure you are not either intentionally or inadvertently infringing copyright. Chapter 5 discusses copyright issues in further detail.

4. *Protect your Web page.* If you have taken the time to create a unique Web page, you should also take the time to ensure it is adequately protected. This includes using a proper copyright notice and perhaps even registering a copyright claim. The threat of copyright infringement is a critical concern. As an on-line publisher, you may even want to consider having users enter into a general access contract which will govern their rights and responsibilities when accessing your Web page.

A general access contract would deal primarily with two areas. First, the on-line publisher will want to establish a fee for access to information. This fee could, for example, be based on the number of documents reviewed or number of visits to the site. Second, the publisher would want to ensure that his or her copyright is protected and, accordingly, confirmed in the contract.

If you plan to have your Web site created by a Web site developer or designer, you should have a Web site development agreement. See the Tips and Traps section at the end of chapter 4 for a discussion of what to include in your agreement.

4

ELECTRONIC CONTRACTS

Most of us enter into contracts every day. With the current popularity of electronic communications and interest in commercial activity on the Internet, attention has recently been focused on the contractual issues raised by electronic communications.

Contracts are typically formed by either an oral or written agreement. They can also be implied by the conduct of the parties. Business agreements, however, have always been based on formal, signed contracts. Now, with the advent of electronic communications, having a signed contract to confirm a business relationship is not always possible. This raises the question: can a contract be formed by the exchange of electronic communications?

There are additional issues to be considered relating to electronic contracts. For example, how can we be sure that the party we are contracting with is really the party he or she claims to be? With an on-line contract, the parties may never meet each other in person in order to verify this. How do we know when an electronic deal is done? Traditionally, once the parties sign their names to a contract, it is considered to be a binding agreement. Can signatures be created on-line? We will explore these issues in this chapter.

a.   THREE ESSENTIAL CHARACTERISTICS OF A CONTRACT

A binding contract has three essential characteristics. The first two are *offer* and *acceptance.* These terms are ordinarily straightforward in the world of paper, but are less so in the cyber world. For example, what happens if a message is scrambled or sent in error? Does the act of downloading — for example, downloading a software program on a trial basis — constitute acceptance? There is no clear answer, and each case must be decided on its own merits.

The third aspect of a binding contract is *consideration.* In addition to offer and acceptance, something of value must be exchanged between the parties to close the deal. In the off-line world, consideration is usually in the form of money, although it can take other forms such as a barter arrangement or an exchange of services instead of money. In the cyber world, monetary transactions can be problematic, in that payment systems over the Internet are not perceived to be secure. However, a number of electronic cash schemes have been developed utilizing cryptography to help ensure privacy and security of on-line payments. Chapter 2 discusses cryptography in more detail.

b. HOW IS AN ELECTRONIC CONTRACT CREATED?

A valid and binding electronic contract can be created in many ways. It can be created through an exchange of e-mail, by the click of a mouse button, or through a Web site. It can also be created partly through electronic communication and partly through some other means of communication, for example, where an offer is made by e-mail to one person and the acceptance is made by mail or fax. In addition, an increasingly common way to create an on-line contract is via a Web site. For example, a Web site may advertise goods or services that may be purchased by completing and transmitting an on-line order form. Such electronic contracts can be verified by fax or by a printout of the electronic message.

c. LEGAL ASPECTS OF THE ON-LINE CONTRACT

1. Does the contract need to be in writing?

Most provinces in Canada have a Statute of Frauds. The terms of this statute may vary amongst the provinces, but the overall intent and purpose is the same. In short, the statute requires that certain contracts must be in writing and under seal. The reason is that the law recognizes that some transactions are so important that a traditional formal contract — written and signed on paper — is required. In these cases, an electronic contract that has been created through, for example, an exchange of e-mail messages and verification by fax or printout of the electronic message may not be considered sufficient for a binding and enforceable contractual relationship.

What kind of transactions require formal contracts? Contracts for the sale of land, long-term leases, and contracts that cannot be performed within one year must be evidenced in writing. As well, a *guarantee*, where someone will ensure that another person fulfills his or her contractual obligations, must also be evidenced in writing. Someone co-signing on a loan is an example of a guarantee.

If you believe your contractual dealing is one that might fall under the Statute of Frauds, make sure you have a formal signed contract in place. Relying on an exchange of e-mail messages may not be good enough for a binding and enforceable contractual relationship. As well, if the transaction involves a significant exchange of money or if it is one that could expose either party to considerable risk if it is not performed, it is a good idea to have the contract in writing.

However, it is likely that many contracts applying to the ordinary sale of goods will be changed to accommodate electronic transactions. In fact, the Statute of Frauds and the Sale of Goods Act in Ontario have recently been amended to eliminate the writing requirement for on-line transactions such as EDI.

2.   Does the contract need to be signed?

If a contract does not need to be in writing and therefore falls outside the Statute of Frauds, it also does not need to be signed — usually. Remember that outside of the electronic world, many contracts are verbal and, in some cases, contracts can be implied by the conduct of the parties. For example, if the parties exchange correspondence that reveals an intention to enter into contractual relations, that correspondence can form the basis of a contract. This includes electronic correspondence.

Now that we have established that on-line contracts do not always have to be signed is this the end of the issue? Not really. Consumer protection legislation could create a problem for on-line contracts. For example, the Ontario Consumer Protection Act provides that in the case of an executory contract, that is, a contract in which payment is made after the contract is entered into, the contract must be signed and each party must have a duplicate original.

One way to get around this potential hurdle could be for the parties to acknowledge that they will each keep a signed hard copy of the electronic contract. At this point, there are no guarantees that this will get around the problem. The matter will have to be sorted out by a revision to the legislation or an actual court case.

It will often not be possible or practical for two or more parties to sign a hard copy version of the contract when it is transmitted electronically. The parties to an electronic contract should include a term in the contract allowing it be to signed in *counterpart*. This legal term means that the parties may sign copies of the contract independently without losing the contract's binding effect.

However, remember that consumer protection legislation is a provincial matter and may vary from province to province. You could check your provincial government's on-line statutes if you are interested in looking into this issue further.

Further, signatures authenticate — or confirm — a contract; they are unique marks that confirm the commitment of the signees of the contract to the relationship. So even though you may not technically need a signature for your electronic contract to be valid, a signature does demonstrate exactly which terms of the contract have been agreed to. It also provides extra assurance and may be well worth having in case a dispute arises.

How can you get a signature for an electronic contract?

(a) Have the contract confirmed by a hard copy or receipt. However, this defeats the purpose of on-line communications by creating paperwork. The time and effort it takes to confirm the transaction by paper raises the question of why have an on-line contract in the first place?

(b) Send an e-mail to the person who has accepted your offer, confirming the terms of the transaction. An e-mail message, however, is insufficient to bind the other person unless he or she sends a response.

(c) Use a digital signature. This solution has been adopted by several jurisdictions in the United States where requirements for signatures on legal documents are stricter than in Canada. A digital signature is not a digital image of a handwritten signature; it is a digital substitute for a manual signature. A digital signature is a unique identifier created using encryption software. See chapter 2 for a discussion of encryption.

To sign an electronic communication, the sender runs the encryption program which creates that identifier. The program encrypts the document. The result is a fully encrypted document with a unique digital signature. The digital signature offers proof of the sender's identity and that the contract has not been altered. The original document together with the digital signature is sent to the intended recipient who can decipher the signature using the same software.

Digital signatures can also be used with other documents such as on-line purchase orders or regular e-mail messages. Digital signatures look different on every document you send on-line and they can't be duplicated.

There are a number of other technology-based ways of ensuring the authentication of electronic communications. Software is available that can identify a document with a digital watermark. Outside of the digital world, watermarks on paper can help prevent counterfeiting and ensure the authenticity of information in documents on which the watermark appears. A digital watermark works in the same way. It is an unique identifier that can name a copyright owner and provide further information about the source and authenticity of the document. Digital watermarks are especially useful to digitized songs and video clips. The digital identifier prevents unauthorized distribution of the work by the person to whom it is sold because it cannot be removed from the electronic document in which it is embedded. In this way it prevents distribution by someone claiming the document as his or her own work.

3.   Which law applies?

Suppose you order a computer from a company located in California. You place the order via the Internet by completing an electronic order form and sending it electronically to the company. The computer you order is delivered to you. Shortly after your purchase you experience many problems with the product, and you want to return it. The company refuses to take it back.

What can you do? If you are thinking about going to court to resolve your dispute, you will need to consider which set of laws will apply in resolving the dispute — the law of the State of California or the law of your province?

When there is a conflict of law, deciding which law applies can be a difficult issue. The law can be complicated. As a general rule, the jurisdiction with the most significant relationship to the facts of the case will be the controlling jurisdiction. A determination of which jurisdiction has the most significant relationship involves an analysis of the place the contract was formulated and the location of the parties, among other things.

If you are considering purchasing goods on-line of substantial worth, the following advice will be helpful:

- Avoid the uncertainty over the jurisdiction issue by specifying in your on-line contract which law will control the dispute in the event of a problem.

- Find out whether or not the company you are dealing with has dealers or subsidiaries near you which would be able to deal with the problem if one arises.

- If you are considering offering a product or service internationally through on-line transactions, obtain advice from a lawyer about the ways a foreign country's laws could affect such transactions. You need to not only know which law would apply if there is a problem but also ensure you are not breaching any foreign laws by making your product or service available to an international audience.

d. DRAFTING YOUR OWN ELECTRONIC CONTRACT

Bearing in mind the above discussion regarding the necessity for contracts to be in writing, and the special issue of electronic signatures, electronic contracts are really not all that different from traditional hard copy contracts. In addition, the clauses in electronic contracts are usually the same as for other contracts.

1. Identify the parties

State the name and address of each of the parties as well as the names that the parties will be referred to within the contract — this often makes it easier for you to draft the agreement. For example, ABC Acceptance Corporation, Inc., can be referred to as ABC in your contract.

2. Describe the services to be provided

Describe as specifically as possible the services or goods that each party is to provide. Do not use open-ended descriptions or indicate that exact services will be mutually agreed on at a later date. These kinds of clauses in a contract will leave you vulnerable to problems later on.

3. Describe the responsibilities of each of the parties

You might also want to describe what will happen if a party does not fulfill his or her responsibility. For example, you could include a term requiring one party to refund money, or a term bringing the contract to an end if there is a severe breach of the contract. Make sure you also specify all deadlines involved in the project and, if applicable, reasonable grace periods.

4. Terms of agreement

Make sure you set out the day on which the agreement is to start as not all agreements start on the day they are signed. If your agreement requires work to be done at several stages, make sure those dates are explicitly set out in your contract. Also, make sure that the termination date for the agreement is set out in writing.

5. Payment terms

Both parties will obviously be very interested in this term. Make sure you deal with any provisions stipulating the terms of credit in a careful, detailed manner. Most provinces have consumer protection laws requiring full disclosure of lending terms and interest rates. You may also want to consider including specific terms dealing with penalties or interest to be imposed for late performance.

6. Performance deadlines

Specify all relevant performance deadlines and detailed procedures for periodic review and approval of services by your customer.

7. Performance criteria

Include terms and procedures for correcting deficient performance and remedying deficient work products or goods.

8.   Warranties

You will want to have the party you are dealing with give you a warranty of the quality of the services and goods it will provide. All services and goods should meet prescribed standards and specifications. In addition, you will want to include procedures for obtaining relief if the services or goods do not meet the warranty.

9.   Default

If the contract cannot be performed, you should be able to rely on this section to enforce the terms of the contract with as little turmoil as possible. This is particularly important if the contract is going to be performed over a long period. You might also wish to deal with the situation where one party becomes bankrupt or is otherwise unable to perform the contract. Lastly, you might also wish to deal with the return of all your data and other materials in the event of a default.

10.   Non-disclosure

Set out all restrictions regarding disclosure for all parties. See chapter 8 for a further discussion of privacy of information.

11.   Modifications to service

Many on-line contracts, such as Web site development agreements (see Tips and Traps section at the end of this chapter), contemplate an ongoing business relationship with the other party. Specify what the terms of that ongoing relationship will be.

CREATING A PROFESSIONAL CONTRACT

1. *Type your contract on standard 8½" x 11" paper.* Number the paragraphs consecutively and use subheadings to identify each separate aspect of the agreement.

2. *Do not use legalese.* Words such as *herein* and *notwithstanding* are vague and tend to confuse the issues. If you are not sure what the word means, find out. In most cases you will find that a complicated legal term can be replaced with plain language.

3. *Use precedents.* There are many available precedents for computer contracts as well as on-line contracts. These precedents can be found in print and, more importantly, on the Internet. Check your local library for legal precedents in the legal reference section. You may also want to check out some of the Web sites referred to later in this book in chapter 10 on legal research on the Internet. Be careful about using precedents, though: not all precedents will apply to your particular case.

Formulate your contract carefully so that it directly applies to your situation. Lawyers have often been accused of being slaves to precedents when they include clauses in agreements which do not really apply to that particular situation. Do not fall into that trap.

4. *Number the pages.* If your contract is lengthy, it will probably contain a number of cross-references to different pages. Marking the pages of your contract 1 of 7, 2 of 7 will ensure that each party knows how many pages are contained in the contract as a whole and it will be immediately obvious if any pages are missing.

5. *Check your contract for mistakes.* It may be too late to correct a problem once your contract is signed. When your draft contract is completed, clearly mark it DRAFT so that you will not get the final contract confused with the original draft. If there is more than one draft, use labels like Draft 1 and Draft 2. Read the draft contract thoroughly and get rid of any excess words or clauses, then retype it.

6. *Copy and read the contract.* Once the contract has been agreed to, make the necessary copies for all the parties involved. If there are three parties to the contract you will want to have at least three clean copies of the contract. Read over the contract one last time before you sign it. If there are any handwritten changes that are made after the contract was copied, be sure each party initials the changes. This helps to avoid the situation where one party claims that the changes were added at a later date without their knowledge.

7. *Sign the contract.* Once the contract is ready to be signed, make sure that all parties sign and date all copies of the contract. If you are dealing with a corporation, be especially attentive. Corporations do business through directors and officers, and it is these individuals who are specifically authorized to make agreements on behalf of the corporation. Unless expressly authorized, no other person can do business on behalf of the corporation. Using the following signature block is a good idea when dealing with a corporation:

ABC CORPORATION by:_____ (name)

I have authority to bind the corporation.

Title:_____

Date:_____

Your contract is now completed.

8. *Keep your copy of the contract safe.* Before storing your contract in a safe place, review it one last time to make note of any significant dates. For example, if the contract is for a term of one year, it might be a good idea to make a note to review it again in 11 months for the purpose of renewal. You will then want to keep a copy of the contract at home in case the original is lost or destroyed. If you have a lawyer, and he or she has a general file open for your company, you might also want to send a copy to him or her for further safekeeping.

9. *Modifying your contract.* Most contracts contain a clause stating that any changes to the contract must be in writing and signed by both parties. This is a good idea as it anticipates a situation where one party attempts to breach the terms of the contract. If a change needs to be made, state exactly what the change is in a new contract, making sure that the new contract will not take the place of the old one. In other words, make sure that your agreement merely *modifies* the old one and does not replace it. Sign and date this contract and keep it together with the original. The best way to ensure that the

modification is not treated as a new contract is to use wording such as:

"This is a modification to a contract titled 'On-line Service Agreement' that was signed by the parties to this agreement on April 13, 1996."

TIPS AND TRAPS

WEB SITE DEVELOPMENT AGREEMENTS

Setting up a home page on the World Wide Web has become a priority for many businesses and organizations hoping to establish a presence on the Internet. The style of Web pages on the Internet varies greatly, from a single page containing perhaps 100 words with no graphics or visual elements to a complicated multi-page site configured with up-to-date specifications including graphics, on-line video, sound recordings, and text displayed in real time.

> The term real time refers to the ability to do things interactively. For example, real time can refer to the ability of two people to do things simultaneously while interacting with one another, even if they are thousands of kilometres apart. Real-time applications on the Internet have become possible in recent years because of the introduction of very powerful programming tools.

The design of your company's Web site and ongoing maintenance services can cost hundreds to thousands of dollars, so it is a good idea to have a formal contract in place governing your rights and responsibilities and those of the Web site developer.

An excellent example of a Web site development agreement can be found at www.kslaw.com/menu by choosing "agr.htm." This is a sample agreement entered into between

King and Spalding, a Georgia law firm, and Cybernet Communications, a Web site developer. The sample contract shown
on the Web site is fairly comprehensive and will give you an
idea of the terms used in a typical Web site development
agreement.

If you intend to draft your own agreement, consider the
following:

1. The speed and downloadability of a Web page is
important. A common complaint of Internet users is
that it takes too long to download a Web page if it
has some combination of text, graphics, music, and
video. You want to avoid a situation where users
become frustrated with having to wait for your page
to be downloaded onto their computer. Specify a
maximum download time for your Web page in the
development agreement.

2. Once your Web page is completed, you will want it
to be readily accessible. The way that most users are
going to find your Web page is through a search
engine such as AltaVista, Yahoo!, Lycos, or Infoseek.
Your developer should make sure that your Web site
address is listed with these, as well as other on-line
search engines. Stipulate this in the agreement.

3. You will need to ensure that your Web site is compatible with the latest versions of Internet browsing
software. At the time this book was printed, Microsoft Explorer and Netscape Navigator occupy the

vast majority of the marketplace. Protect yourself with a clause requiring this current compatibility.

4. Web pages often have links to other, related Web pages. For example, if you have a Web page for promoting your compact disc store, you may want to have links to the Web pages of musical artists, record companies, concert listings, or music magazines.

However, in a recent U.S. case involving Microsoft, the generally accepted practice of linking to another Web site without permission was challenged. In January 1999, Ticketmaster and Microsoft settled their two-year-old lawsuit. As a result of the settlement and an agreement between the parties not to disclose any of the settlement terms, those in the industry looking for the U.S. federal court's guidance on the issue of linking were disappointed.

As we'll discuss later in the book, although U.S. law is obviously not binding on Canadian courts, the United States has many more Internet-related statutes and rules, and often deals with issues that have not yet been put before the Canadian court system.

Also, because of the international scope of cyberspace, you need to be aware of not only Canadian law but also international laws. For this reason, it is important and useful for Canadians to be aware of the issues raised in the Microsoft case.

Whether or not this case truly involves a copyright issue is disputed. Most commentators believe that it is not a copyright issue because it simply involves the copying of an Internet address. An analogy of the situation has been drawn to the publisher of a telephone book who lists the addresses of local citizens. However, regardless of the copyright question, it is now common practice to get the permission from someone before linking to his or her Web page. The Tips and Traps section of chapter 5 discusses this issue further.

It is a good idea to stipulate that your Web site developer be responsible for obtaining permission from those persons or companies you wish to offer links to in your Web page. Your Web developer should also be obliged to obtain the rights to use other works that are to be included in your Web site and which may be copyrighted. Such works may be photographs, sound recordings, or graphics. To obtain those rights, the owner must be identified and permission obtained.

It is important to note that if your agreement with a Web site developer requires him or her to get copyright permission on your behalf and, unknown to you, the permission is not obtained, you will still be responsible for any copyright infringement. However, you will be able to make a claim against the Web site developer for any damages you may have to pay as a result of the infringement.

5. You should make sure that your Web site is portable. ISPs are facing a rather uncertain future with the recent entry of national telecommunications companies such as Rogers Cable and Bell into the market. If your ISP has also designed your Web site, as many do in addition to providing hosting services, include a clause in your Web site development agreement requiring that your ISP make reasonable efforts to transfer your domain name to another ISP at your request. You should consider making such a transfer as soon as you see any warning signs. For example, if the ISP no longer has staff available to answer your telephone inquiries or you begin to experience frequent or prolonged periods of downtime.

If your Web developer is not your ISP, a portability clause should be included in your contract with the ISP.

You will also want to obtain all your original content from the ISP or Web site developer if a problem arises. Include a clause in your contract requiring delivery of your original material — e.g., graphic files, video, and music recordings — within a specified period on demand.

6. The contract should contemplate an ongoing business relationship with the Web site developer. Your site might need frequent updating or changes. Specify what the terms of your ongoing relationship will be.

5

WHO OWNS WHAT IN CYBERSPACE?

a. WHAT IS COPYRIGHT?

Copyright is a form of protection for those who create original works. It would not be fair, for example, for someone to copy your computer program without your permission and sell it to others. As the creator of the program, you have certain legal rights, the most important being the right to prohibit others from copying your work without your permission.

Copyright is often confused with trademark and patent; although related, the concepts are quite different. Trademarks are typically used to protect brand names, while patents usually apply to inventions.

In Canada, copyright law is governed by a federal statute called the Copyright Act. The Copyright Act has been around for many years and is designed to protect authors of works such as magazine articles, books, paintings, drawings, dramatic works, photographs, films, and musical works.

The difficulty with the Copyright Act is adapting its provisions to the modern world of computer communications. There is no question that copyright protection extends to computer software. In the words of one Canadian judge, "Creating a new software package with stolen parts is akin to removing components from an employer's warehouse in a lunch pail and attempting to sell the assembled product."

It would also seem that copyright extends to works displayed on-line. After all, copyright encompasses all forms of written expressions, including sound recordings of those writings.

It has been said that the World Wide Web is the world's largest photocopier and, as such, the opportunities for copyright infringement abound. It is easy to make a copy of information in digital form without being detected and to then modify that copy for your own personal gain. For example, it is a fairly simple procedure to copy the basic code from a computer program and modify the program slightly to pass it off as your own.

Consequently, it has become easy to infringe copyright in the digital world, sometimes on a massive scale. The world of on-line communications poses perhaps the greatest challenge to our laws of copyright protection. To understand how copyright may be infringed, we need to know what is protected by copyright.

b.   WHAT IS PROTECTED BY COPYRIGHT?

The Copyright Act protects virtually all types of information on the Internet. If something is considered an original work, it is protected by the Copyright Act. Work is the term used in the Copyright Act and is broadly defined. It is important to note, however, that while the Copyright Act protects the form of expression of an idea, it does not protect the idea itself.

(a) *Literary works.* All types of written works such as articles, books, and poems are protected by the Copyright Act. If something is expressed in words, numbers or other symbols, it can most likely be copyrighted. Most of the works available on the Internet would probably qualify as literary works. For example, information posted to bulletin boards and appearing on Web pages would likely qualify as a literary works and therefore be entitled to copyright protection.

(b) *Data or facts.* As a general rule, data or facts cannot be copyrighted. This is, however, a gray area. Take, for example, someone who assembles a list of the names of all the lawyers in Quebec and then sells that list for a profit. While there may be some copyright protection in the actual form of the directory, there is no copyright protection for the addresses and information about each of the lawyers. The copyright protection, in this case, is in the way the facts are presented.

(c) *Computer programs.* There is no question that computer programs are protected by copyright law. The explicit protection of computer programs came in an amendment to the Copyright Act made in 1988. The Copyright Act defines a computer program as "a set of instructions or statements expressed, fixed, embodied, or stored in any manner, that is to be used directly or indirectly in a computer in order to bring about a specific result." As you would expect, the language used to write the computer program is not protected by copyright.

(d) *Sound recordings.* Sound recordings, including musical recordings, recordings of dramatic works, and sound effects, can all be copyrighted.

COMBATTING ON-LINE MUSIC PIRATES

The development of a new technology called MP3 has caused the big record companies a great deal of concern. Why? MP3 permits a user to download music from the Internet to a small hardware device costing no more than $300. A number of on-line pirates have used MP3 technology to distribute sound recordings in the Internet without payment of royalties to the record companies. The result? The recording industry is scrambling to develop its own technical standard for the copyrighted sale and digital delivery of music over the Internet.

(e) *Multimedia works.* Multimedia is a combination of work in two or more mediums. For example, a Web page with graphic images, text, and video qualifies as a multimedia work. Just because the Web page incorporates more than one type of image does not take away from the protection that is afforded from the Copyright Act. The work as a whole is thoroughly protected.

(f) *Blank forms or templates.* You will encounter sample forms all over the Internet. Several of the Web sites referred to in this book contain sample legal forms and precedents. Are these legal forms protected by copyright? The answer is probably yes.

The question to ask yourself is whether or not there was some judgment, skill, or labour used in preparing the form. If so, the form is likely protected by copyright. On the other hand, if the form is merely a copy of another form (a copy of a tax form, for example), it may not be copyrighted.

(g) *Fictional characters.* Fictional characters include both visual representations (e.g., Mickey Mouse and Popeye) and characters in literary works (e.g., Sherlock Holmes or Captain Bligh). If the character is a visual representation, the image of the character is likely able to be copyrighted because the image of the character is a unique and distinct expression of an idea.

The name of the character may also be protected by copyright. Take a Sherlock Holmes novel for example. Clearly, Sherlock Holmes and Watson are well-developed key characters within the story, and as such are critical to the book as a whole. Lesser-known or minor characters, however, are not able to be copyrighted because that character does not sufficiently possess original and distinctive characteristics.

For a work to be copyrightable, certain technical requirements of the Copyright Act must be met. First, the creator of the work must be a Canadian citizen or subject of the Commonwealth or a citizen of a country adhering to the Berne Convention. The Berne Convention is an international treaty entered into by most of the world's industrialized nations which allows for copyright protection similar to that under the Canadian Copyright Act.

The Copyright Act also requires that the work must be fixed in some permanent way, for example, the work must be in writing, displayed in some sort of permanent presentation, or recorded on film or video tape. Being original is not enough. It makes no difference what the form of the work is as long as the information can be read, heard, or viewed directly through the use of a machine or device such as a computer or CD player. Information fixed in a digital form on floppy computer disk, hard drive, or CD ROM meets the fixation requirement necessary for copyright protection. Canadian courts have not yet ruled on information created for placement on an electronic database, Web site, or File Transfer Protocol site.

FILE TRANSFER PROTOCOL (FTP)

FTP is an Internet application which allows you to transfer files from a remote computer to your personal computer. Files can include documents, photographs, and computer software. There are hundreds of sites on the Internet that store files and let you connect using FTP to import those files to your computer.

United States courts have ruled that even a computer program residing in the random access memory (RAM) of a computer for only a millisecond is sufficiently fixed to meet the requirements of the U.S. equivalent of our Copyright Act.

c. HOW IS COPYRIGHT OBTAINED?

Copyright is automatic. An original work is protected by copyright at the time that work is created and usually continues until 50 years after the author of the work dies.

There is no formal requirement to register a copyright, although you can register it in Canada at the Canadian Copyright Office in Ottawa. Registration provides the benefit of establishing the date on which the original work was completed. For example, if two authors of a similarly worded manuscript enter into a dispute about who the creator of the work actually is, the person who is able to prove with some certainty the date on which the document was created will have an advantage.

One simple way of establishing the date on which your work was created is to mail the original work to yourself in a self-addressed envelope. The envelope will, of course, be post-marked with the date on which it was mailed, and can be used as proof that you wrote the work on or before the postal registration date. Do not open the package once you receive it in the mail.

You can notify others of your copyright in a work by marking it with a copyright notice: copyright by Jack & Jill Limited, 1997. The notice can be simple, displaying the copyright symbol (©) followed by the name of the copyright owner and the year in which the work was established: © Jack & Jill Limited, 1997.

The notice can also be more detailed, like that of the Law Society of Upper Canada's copyright and disclaimer notice, which is reproduced below (with permission, of course):

Intellectual Property Notice

Copyright © 1996 Law Society of Upper Canada. All rights reserved. Law Society of Upper Canada either owns the intellectual property rights in the underlying HTML, text, audio clips, video clips, and other content that is made available to you on this Home Page, or has obtained the permission of the owner of the intellectual property in such content to use the content on this Home Page.

Limited Licence

❑ Law Society of Upper Canada grants to you a limited licence to display on your computer, print, download, and use this underlying HTML, text, audio clips, video clips, and other content that is made available to you on this Home Page, for non-commercial, personal, or educational purposes only, provided that:

❑ you do not modify any such content, and

❑ you include with and display on each copy of such content the associated copyright notice and this limited license.

❑ Notwithstanding the above limitations, members of the Law Society may make appropriate use of this material in their professional practice.

❑ No other use is permitted. Without limiting the generality of the forgoing, you may not:

❑ make any commercial use of such content;

❑ include such content in or with any product that you create or distribute;

or

❑ copy such content onto your or any other person's World Wide Web Home Page. Nothing contained in this Section shall be construed as conferring any right in any copyright of the Law Society of Upper Canada or any other person who owns the copyright in content provided on this Home Page.

You can visit the Law Society's Web site at www.lsuc.on.ca.

d.   WHAT ARE YOUR COPY RIGHTS?

The most obvious right of an owner of copyright is the right to make copies of his or her original work. In addition to the right to copy the work, the owner also has what is commonly referred to as a bundle of rights, which are often specific to the type of work. For example, in the case of a computer program, the bundle of rights includes the right to rent or license the software to others. The following is the bundle of rights with respect to digital information:

(a) *The right to make copies.* This can be a difficult issue when we are dealing with computerized information. For example, does the sending of an e-mail message constitute making a copy? On an even broader scale, whenever a computer user accesses a document on another computer — i.e., on a computer network — information is reproduced. In fact, when you really think about it, it is almost impossible to do anything on-line without making a copy. Accordingly, in the absence of permission from the copyright owner, the copying of such information constitutes a copyright infringement (we will discuss copyright infringement later in this chapter in section **i.**). Applying the general to the specific, the following acts, then, may constitute making a copy:

- Browsing or viewing a document from another computer. This involves the transfer of information from hard storage — a hard disk, diskette, or CD ROM — to your computer memory in order to display information.

- Downloading computer files from one computer system — for example downloading a file, Web site — to another computer system.

- Digitally sampling a copyrighted sound recording and using it for your own purpose.

- Scanning a photograph or drawing.

(b) *The right to assign or license the use of a work.* Copyright of a work may be assigned or licensed to others. An assignment, or transfer, of copyright must be in writing to be effective.

ELECTRONIC RIGHTS

Electronic rights are extremely wide ranging. Many older contracts contain rather vaguely worded clauses about electronic rights of reproduction, almost as an afterthought. Subsequently, both authors and publishers are often faced with the question of who owns electronic rights to the material. For example, does a publishing contract permit the publisher to put a sample chapter of the author's work on the publisher's Web site? If the contract includes licensing of electronic rights to the publisher, the answer is yes. Unfortunately, the answer is not always so clear cut.

(c) *Distribution right.* The Copyright Act gives the owner the exclusive right to distribute the copyrighted work. This includes the right to sell copies of the work, as well as the right to rent, lend, or license copies of the work.

It is important to understand the difference between the right to distribute and the right to assign. The right to distribute generally involves the transfer of one copy for a person's use. With an assignment of copyright, the person to whom the right is assigned acquires, more or less, the rights of the original copyright owner.

(d) *Adaptation right.* A copyright owner also has the exclusive right to make changes to the original work.

Works based on the original work, called derivative works, are given the same protection as the original work. For example, a French translation of a computerized spell check program which has been translated or authorized for translation by the copyright owner is a derivative work and is afforded the same protection as the original program.

The right to adapt works is critical in on-line communications simply because of the ease with which digital information may be digitally modified or incorporated into other works. Modifying or adapting a copyrighted work is as much an infringement as using the original work without the copyright owner's permission. There are some exceptions to this rule; these are discussed in section i. on copyright infringement. For example, using another person's source code (the computer language which forms the basis for a document or program) in your own program which, even if modified, is similar to the original work, is illegal.

(e) *Protecting Derivative Work.* As we discussed above, a copyright holder has the exclusive right to make derivative works on a copyrighted work. A derivative work is one which is based upon one or more preexisting works. This issue was recently tested in a U.S. case involving FormGen Incorporated, the maker of the popular computer game, Duke Nukem 3D. The purpose of this game is to zap evil aliens while searching for a secret passage to the next level. The game has 29 levels and a "build editor" which enables players to create their own levels. New levels are usually posted on the Internet and downloaded by other players for free.

A distributor of software, Microstar, decided to collect the user-created levels and sell them in a CD version titled, Nuke It. The parties ended up in court. The major issue to be decided was whether Microstar's sale of Nuke It infringed FormGen's right to make derivative works based on Duke Nukem. The court sided with FormGen and, in doing so, spelled out several important principles which are equally applicable in Canadian law, namely:

- The copyright protection on a computer game of other fictitious work is not limited to the nuts and bolts of the computer's code and graphic images. The protection extends to the "story" and "look and feel" of the program.

- A copyright owner has the exclusive right to create sequels based on the copyrighted work. Accordingly, anyone who creates a sequel to a copyrighted work without getting permission is likely to be sued for infringement.

(f) *Public performance right.* Owners of copyrighted works also have the exclusive right to perform their works publicly. In the case of digital communications, it may be a breach of the Copyright Act if someone displays a CD ROM or digital image to a large public group. For example, a professor wishing to display images from a CD ROM to a classroom of hundreds of students must obtain permission from the copyright owner to do so.

(g) *Moral rights.* Moral rights are personal and are said to attach to the actual personality of the artist or creator of the unique work. Moral rights are retained by the artist even after he or she has sold or assigned the actual work. The concept of moral rights is a simple one. They are designed to protect the integrity of the work after publication. So, for example, an author can prevent the use of the work in association with another product or service: an author can invoke his or her moral rights to prevent a fictional character he or she has created from being associated with cigarettes. The author can also prevent certain changes or modifications being made to the original work.

Moral rights also protect the identity of the author by allowing the author to be associated with the work or, on the other hand, remain anonymous or use a pen name in association with the work.

e. LIMITATIONS ON COPYRIGHT

The Copyright Act contains a number of exceptions to the general rule that a work cannot be used in whole or in part without the permission of the copyright owner. One example is the *fair dealing* exception. The principle itself is straightforward. If the court considers the infringement to be fair and the use falls into one of a number of categories, that use will not be considered to be a breach of the Copyright Act. Accordingly, the use of otherwise copyrighted material for private study, research, or criticism is acceptable.

What is not so straightforward, however, is determining whether the infringement is indeed fair. As well, the fair dealing exception has been refined by a recent amendment to the Act. Now in many cases the author of the work must be cited for the use to be considered fair dealing.

The use of copyrighted material is also acceptable if such use is with the explicit or implied permission of the copyright owner.

By applying the exceptions outlined above — private study, research, or criticism — it is easy to see that not all on-line copying of digital information necessarily constitutes copyright infringement. It may be also be possible to argue that certain forms of copying that might otherwise be unacceptable are perfectly acceptable in the digital world.

One such example is the sending and receiving of e-mail messages which, of course, involves the copying of information from one computer to another. Although the forwarding of an e-mail message originally sent to you by another person might be a copyright infringement, the generally accepted custom implies that such use is acceptable. Unfortunately, there have been no Canadian cases to guide us as to what is fair in cyberspace.

What about copyright on the World Wide Web? Just because someone has incorporated an image or text into his or her Web page does not mean he or she has authorized use of that information. Be careful about copying elements from other Web pages and using them for yourself.

Some places on the Internet not only permit people to copy original works from the sites but invite people to do so. There are a number of Web sites containing graphic and photographic images which you may incorporate into your Web page. Similarly, if someone puts a file on a File Transfer Protocol site (FTP), it is implied that he or she is inviting others to download that file for use, as this is the very purpose of FTP. However, if you are in doubt, get permission from the copyright owner.

f.   COMMON MISCONCEPTIONS ABOUT COPYRIGHT

The following list of myths and facts illustrates some of the many common mistakes that people make regarding copyright.

Myth: It is okay to copy information as long as I do not make any money from it.

Fact: Wrong. Just because you are not using the information for commercial purposes does not mean that it is okay to copy it without permission.

Consider a 1993 U.S. case involving Playboy Enterprises. Playboy sued the operator of a computer bulletin board for making digitized photos of Playboy models available to its subscribers. These images were copied from Playboy magazines without Playboy's consent. Although the bulletin board operator did not charge for the photographs, he did charge a monthly subscription fee to the bulletin board. The court found this to be a significant factor and ruled that the use of the photographs by the bulletin board operator was unfair.

The same result would likely occur in Canada. In fact, it has been reported that two Canadian bulletin board operators who were making copyrighted information available for distribution in their respective services have pleaded guilty to charges under the Copyright Act.

Similarly, it is not acceptable to infringe copyright even if your use is not for profit. Even if you intend to use copyrighted material for only personal or educational purposes, you must still give proper attribution to the copyright owner. The failure to do so in these types of cases can result in a suit for plagiarism, an issue quite separate from copyright infringement, though serious nonetheless. Plagiarism involves passing off another person's ideas as your own.

Myth: If everyone does it, it is okay. It is okay to use copyrighted information without permission from the author if other people do so.

Fact: Maybe. The issue of whether or not there is an implied right to use copyrighted information through custom and practice is not easy to ascertain. Consider the practice of videotaping copyrighted movies from the television. Everyone does it, but is it legal? It was only after the U.S. Supreme Court determined that home videotaping, or taping for personal use was legal that this particular copyright issue was settled.

Myth: It is acceptable to copy only a small portion of a copyrighted work.

Fact: Copying a small portion of a copyrighted work may still be infringement if what you are copying is the heart and soul of the work. Remember that the purpose of copyright protection is to protect the expression of an original idea. If the material you are copying contains the basic and essential element of the work, it is likely that you are guilty of copyright infringement. If you want your use to be considered fair, use as little as possible of the original work. Don't copy word for word and don't use direct quotations unless you properly acknowledge the author.

Myth: I am allowed to make a copy of a program for backup purposes.

Fact: Provided you are using the original copy of the computer program with authorization, you may copy that program for backup purposes. Bear in mind, however, that this exception is limited to a *single* reproduction of the program.

Myth: It is okay to make minor modifications to a program to make it compatible with my system.

Fact: Again, the Copyright Act says this practice is not an infringement if:

- you can show that the reproduction is essential for the compatibility of the computer program with your computer,

- the reproduction is solely for your own use, and

- the reproduction is destroyed immediately once you relinquish ownership of your copy of the computer program.

Myth: It is okay to copy this information because there is no copyright notice.

Fact: Wrong. The absence of a copyright notice or the failure of the copyright owner to register his or her work does not mean that it is permissible for you to copy it. Copyright protection applies automatically so long as the information or documentation falls within the definition of a work as defined and protected by the Copyright Act.

Myth: If an original work is created by my employee, it belongs to me.

Fact: Usually, a copyrighted work produced by an employee is considered to be owned by the employer. To avoid any confusion, it might be a good idea to enter into a written contract dealing specifically with this issue.

Myth: I am not infringing copyright if I use the programming codes of someone else's Web page as a template for my own Web page. (This is easily accomplished by accessing the hypertext mark-up language — HTML — of the existing Web page and copying these HTML codes for your own. The HTML codes are used to create the graphic and textual interface on a Web page, dictating how the finished page will look.)

Fact: Is this practice a breach of copyright? It depends. In theory, you have already breached copyright by downloading the code of the Web page from the Web server on which the Web page resides to the memory of your own computer. However, this is common and accepted practice, and accordingly would not be considered a violation of copyright law.

Although there is no written exception in law that permits the copying of a Web page into the memory of your computer, this practice is the essence of how people look at and use Web sites on the Internet. If this practice were not allowed, it would be impossible to view documents on the World Wide Web.

The situation can become more complicated. Consider the following two scenarios:

(a) You have very little experience designing a Web page and decide to copy a very simple Web page which contains no graphics or other unusual features. You strip out all the original text from the existing Web page, leaving only the HTML codes. You then substitute your own text. This case is unlikely to be considered a breach of copyright. You have not really made use of any original ideas and are only using the HTML codes for simplicity and ease of use.

(b) You create your own Web page from a very complicated and unusual Web page which contains sound recordings, video clips, and interesting graphic images. You have used similar colours, fonts, and graphics to the existing Web page in your own page. Although this exact scenario has not been considered by Canadian courts, it is quite possible that your use of many of the details and style of this very distinctive Web page could be a breach of copyright.

Myth: A violation of copyright law is not really a serious offense.

Fact: Wrong. The Copyright Act provides for very stiff penalties including substantial fines and/or impoundment or destruction of infringing copies. In addition to the quasi-criminal sanctions set out in the Copyright Act, you could also be subject to a civil suit which could result in your having to pay damages, among other things.

Myth: As long as I give credit to the owner of the copyrighted work I can use it.

Fact: Simply giving credit is not enough. The Copyright Act goes beyond requiring that credit be given to the author of an original idea. You must get permission from the owner of the work in order to use the work.

g.   SOFTWARE PIRACY

The Internet is a tempting place for software pirates. With so much free information available on the Web, people often get the impression that they can take what they like. Sometimes they are right.

For example, many companies encourage you to download software from the Internet at no cost. The software may support products that they sell such as drivers or corrections for bugs that have developed in their products. However, most software is subject to copyright protection, making it illegal to copy certain types of software programs without the owner's consent.

While most people have general notions of what copyright law is all about, many don't realize that a breach of copyright is a criminal offence punishable by severe penalties. In 1988, parliament amended the Canadian Copyright Act to expressly include computer programs in the definition of literary works, thereby confirming that software is eligible for copyright protection and prohibiting the unauthorized copying of software programs without the consent of the copyright owner.

There are exceptions to the rule. For example, it is not an offence to make a backup copy of your software program. Nor is it an offence to adapt a program to another computer language to make it compatible with your computer. Most of these exceptions are, however, limited to a single copy for personal use.

The Copyright Act also makes it an offence to knowingly produce or distribute copies of computer programs for sale. On January 1, 1994, a loophole in the Copyright Act was plugged with the addition of an amendment making the rental of a software program a copyright infringement.

A breach of the provisions of the Copyright Act is a serious matter. Just because the provisions are not covered by the Criminal Code, does not mean that serious penalties do not apply. A breach of the Copyright Act can result in a fine up to $1 000 000, a jail term of up to five years, or both. In addition to a fine and/or imprisonment, you or your company may face an injunction preventing you from conducting business, an award of monetary damages and an accounting of profits.

Every day pirated software is used, either knowingly or unknowingly, by people everywhere. Often it is just simply a case of someone making a copy of a software package — often word-processing software — for a friend. However, there are other instances which involve piracy on a grand scale. For example, a mid-western U.S. university recently discovered some 900 megabytes of its computer storage was occupied by stolen software and that its computer system was being accessed by software thieves from around the world who were downloading copies of stolen software 24 hours a day, 7 days a week. In this case, the software found on the computer was worth several thousands of dollars for each copy. Hundreds of copies were taken by thieves.

It has been estimated that Canada has a piracy rate of approximately 50%, meaning that for every 100 legitimate software programs in use, an estimated 50 or more are illegally obtained copies.

What are your responsibilities as a user? Your first responsibility is to use programs for your own use only. As we discussed above, it is illegal to copy a piece of software. Copying can mean the purchase of a single set of original software and loading it on to more than one computer or modifying an original piece of software to make it available to more than one user, for example, on a network. Most software that is used on a network is sold on a licensing basis. If you wish to have five employees use the software, you must purchase five licences. While the breach of the licence agreement is clearly a breach of software contract and may result in you or your company suffering monetary damages, such a breach could also be considered a violation of the Copyright Act.

In addition to possible criminal and civil liability, there are other risks to using pirated or illegally copied software. Most reputable software developers ensure that the data they provide in the form of software programs is free of viruses. There is no such guarantee when you accept programs which have been copied from another person's computer system. Also, you will not be able to legitimately obtain software upgrades, technical support, or documentation for pirated software.

h. USING COPYRIGHTED MATERIAL

Just because a work is marked with a copyright notice does not mean that you cannot use it for any use that falls outside of fair dealing (see section e. above). You can — you just have to get permission first. How do you go about obtaining permission? It can be a difficult and complicated process and there is no single, infallible way of getting permission to use someone else's material. Sometimes you have to do a bit of hunting.

WHOSE PERMISSION DO YOU NEED?

Text: You need permission from the copyright holder (usually the publisher or the author) or possibly from someone who has been assigned the right.

Photographs: You need permission from the person who took the photograph and possibly from anyone shown in the picture. If the picture contains special logos or trademarks, get permission from the copyright owner of the logos or trademarks as well.

Music: Permission must be obtained from the music publisher, and the performer, and probably from the record company. Fees can vary depending on the performer involved.

Video: You need permission from the maker of the video, the director, if any, and the people featured in the video. This task can be more difficult if the video is also combined with a musical recording.

The first place to check for permission is with the actual owner of the copyrighted material. Try to obtain the name, address, or e-mail address of the copyright owner. You might want to check with the Register at the Copyright Office at the address given below. This office will tell you whether the copyright has been registered in Canada.

Canadian Intellectual Property Office
Industry Canada
Place du Portage, Tower 1
50 Victoria Street
Hull, QC K1A 0C9
Telephone: (819) 997-1725
Fax: (819) 953-6977

The copyright owner does not always have the authority to grant permission; often, this authority is granted to the publisher of the material for the duration of the publishing contract.

You may also wish to check with the Canadian copyright collective. A copyright collective handles requests for permission to use materials on behalf of many different copyright owners. By doing so, the collective offers users of copyrighted materials quick access to a large library of materials.

The Canadian Copyright Licensing Agency, known as CANCOPY, administers the rights to published print materials in Canada (except for Quebec). If you want to use information from a book chapter, newspaper, or magazine, you may obtain a licence to use that information directly from CANCOPY as long as your copying of the information is not a substitute for the purchase of the original work. The e-mail address for CANCOPY is: admin@CANCOPY.com.

If you cannot find the owner of the copyrighted material and CANCOPY cannot help you, you may wish to get in touch with a lawyer to assist you.

If, after all the above efforts, you have failed to obtain a response to your permission request, you may be able to use the copyrighted material without permission from the copyright holder. The Copyright Act sets out a procedure for an application to be made to a board to use material without permission. Typically, the board will examine your efforts to locate and contact the holder of the copyright information. If the board is satisfied that your efforts were exhaustive and reasonable, it will grant you a licence to use the copyrighted information.

Since you obviously cannot make an application to the board every time you are unable to get permission to use a copyrighted work, it is a good idea to protect yourself by making notes of all your efforts to contact the copyright holder by telephone, e-mail messages, and correspondence to the copyright holder. These records will help you prove that you made an exhaustive and reasonable effort to get permission to use the work.

i.   USING SHAREWARE

Shareware is copyrighted computer software which is sold in a way that allows the user to first try out the software before paying for it. Companies offering shareware are common on the Internet. For such companies, offering software on-line is an inexpensive mode of distribution and, in addition, permits such companies to extensively test their software before mass market distribution. Shareware is generally given away for free, but contains a "lock" which prohibits use after a certain time period if payment is not made. If the user chooses to keep a copy of the shareware, the company will provide a key or password permitting indefinite use. Some software is even available on the Internet on a "good faith" basis. In other words, no payment is required. Neither is a key or password required.

This does not mean, though, that shareware can be copied and distributed without the developers express consent, whether or not it is free. Many Internet users have a misconception that copyright protection only extends to software that is purchased over the counter in a box. This is not the case.

Take the example of the recent U.S. case of *Storm Impact Incorporated* versus *Software of the Month Club*. In this case, Storm produced computer shareware game programs. The defendant, Software of the Month Club, distributed Storm's software in one of its monthly compact discs with a recommendation that the software be registered if the recipient enjoyed it. The Club argued that it had a right to distribute Storm's software because it had been posted on the Internet for free distribution. The court rejected this argument and awarded Storm US$20 000.

The impact of this case is clear. The posting of shareware on the Internet does not infer the right to copy and distribute such shareware. If in doubt, obtain permission from the author of the shareware.

j.   WHAT ARE YOUR REMEDIES FOR COPYRIGHT INFRINGEMENT?

A number of different remedies for copyright infringement are available to a copyright owner. The owner might decide to proceed with an injunction to prevent further infringement of the copyright. In addition, damages or monetary compensation may be sought.

Legal action for copyright infringement can be complicated; the services of a lawyer will most certainly be required. The legal proceeding itself can be complicated and involve strict time limitations for proceeding with a claim. For example, a three-year limitation period applies to actions for copyright infringement unless the defendant has fraudulently concealed the acts of infringement.

Civil remedies for copyright infringement are discussed below:

(a) *Injunction.* An injunction can be an effective tool to stop copyright infringement. It is a remedy which can be obtained relatively quickly. If the copyright owner can demonstrate to the court that he or she has a good case at the beginning of the litigation, the court has the power to issue an interlocutory or temporary injunction which will prohibit the action until the litigation is completed.

Once litigation is completed, the court can make the injunction permanent and award other remedies such as damages. However, litigation for injunctive relief can be expensive and risky. If you fail to prove that you are entitled to a permanent injunction, you will be held liable for the defendant's loss of profits and costs of the litigation.

(b) *Ownership of offending copies.* The Copyright Act states that "all infringing copies of any work in which copyright subsists, or of any substantial part thereof, and all plates used or intended to be used for the production of the infringing copies shall be deemed to be the property of the owner of the copyright, who accordingly may take proceedings for the recovery of the possession thereof . . ."

This may also be an effective tool for putting a stop to copyright infringement. For example, if someone copies your ideas and puts them into a book, you will be entitled to all the copies of that book or, alternatively, to reasonable profits that might have otherwise been derived from the sale of the book. For example, if the person who infringed on copyright had printed 5 000 copies of a book and expected a $2 profit per book, he or she could be liable for damages in the amount of $10 000. In addition, that person could also be responsible for general damages as discussed in the next section.

(c) *Damages.* According to the Copyright Act, when a person infringes on the copyright of any work that is protected under the act, that person is liable to pay damages to the owner of the copyright. Those damages might include the copyright owner's loss of profits due to the infringement and part or all of the profits earned from the infringement, as discussed above. Damages may also be awarded for depreciation of the value of the copyright or for damage to the copyright owner's reputation.

(d) *Seizure of imported copies.* Unauthorized copies of work made outside of Canada may be prohibited from importation and seized by Revenue Canada. It is easy to see how this may be a useful remedy in the case of books, which can be physically taken by Revenue Canada officials upon entry into Canada. However, the digital information age poses a number of difficulties to seizure of electronic material. At the moment the free flow of digital information over our borders makes it hard to imagine how Revenue Canada would be able to prohibit the importation of electronic material infringing on Canadian copyright.

Copyright infringement is also punishable by criminal sanction. Stiff penalties exist under both the Copyright Act and the Criminal Code. Those penalties are discussed in more detail in chapter 9 on computer crime.

TIPS AND TRAPS

IS IT OKAY TO LINK TO OTHER PEOPLE'S WEB PAGES WITHOUT THEIR CONSENT?

As discussed in earlier chapters, linking allows Internet users to jump from Web site to Web site. It is a defining characteristic of the Internet and, so far, has been allowed without consent from the owner of the Web page to which the link takes viewers.

However, several recent lawsuits have challenged the notion of being able to create links to other sites without authorization. Most recently, TicketMaster has sued Microsoft for linking without consent to an internal Web page of the ticket company. That suit is still unresolved.

You may want to check out the text of a Georgia state statute limiting unauthorized links. The statute is being challenged by the American Civil Liberties Union. The statute and related documents can be found at www.kuesterlaw.com/kgalaw.

6

TRADEMARKS AND DOMAIN NAMES

a. WHAT IS A TRADEMARK?

A trademark is a word, set of words, or symbol that is used to distinguish the goods or services of one person from those of another. *Compaq* and *IBM* are examples of trademarks in the computer world. Because people identify particular products by their trademark name, the owners of trademarks regard their trademarks as very valuable and naturally want to protect them. *Kleenex* is good example of a valuable, widely recognized trademark. It is, in fact, such a powerful trademark that people often refer to tissue paper as Kleenex.

A trademark does not necessarily have to consist of words and phrases. A drawing can also constitute a trademark, as can pictures and symbols, numerals, nicknames, even colours and sound recordings (as long as they are closely associated with the product). The terms *trademarks* and *trade names* are often used interchangeably. Trademark is a more general term encompassing trade names, and can include names, graphics, logos, and symbols.

The key characteristic of a trademark is that the owner has the exclusive right to use it. For instance, the only company that can sell computers under the name Compaq is the company that has trademarked the name Compaq.

Trademarks can be worth millions of dollars. The right to sell soda pop under the trademark Coca-Cola could be argued to be worth billions of dollars. For this reason, trademark owners will go to great lengths to protect their trademarks.

In Canada, trademark rights are acquired by actually using a trademark in your business practice to distinguish your goods from other people's goods. Although no actual trademark registration is necessary, it is strongly encouraged. Registration of your trademark makes it easier and less expensive for you to enforce your trademark than if it wasn't registered. As well, registration grants nationwide priority, which may be a significant benefit for a business just starting out in a limited geographical area.

Trademarks can be registered with the federal government. The registration is somewhat technical and requires a reproduction of the mark to be filed with the application. Although trademark registration can be completed without a lawyer, it is a good idea to retain one to help you.

b.   USING TRADEMARKS IN CYBERSPACE

Trademarks are used in cyberspace in much the same way as they are in the off-line world. The World Wide Web has become a centre of commercial activity and it is only natural that corporations will want to use their unique trademarks on the Internet when advertising their goods for sale. Trademarks are also becoming more and more important in identifying services offered in cyberspace. For example, Yahoo! is a trademark identifying the Yahoo! search page, and is a name that is now widely recognized. In addition, the trademarking of Internet domain names is becoming increasingly common.

To avoid any confusion about your claim for trademark, it is a good idea to follow these general rules when using trademarks on-line:

- Your unique trademark should be prominently displayed when someone accesses your Web page. Encode your trademark onto your digital product so that it is displayed at least once every time a user views your product. For example, you will see the IBM mark every time you use IBM software. Similarly, you will see the Microsoft mark every time you boot up a version of DOS or Windows.

- Place your mark on all advertising, marketing, and promotions of your goods and/or services.

- Use your trademark as a name of files containing your digital product. For example, if you are downloading files from your Web site, incorporate your trademark into the file name. For example, "ABC.EXE" would signify that you sent a program under your trademark name "ABC."

c. WHAT IS A DOMAIN NAME?

The Internet consists of independent networks containing millions of computers. To get from one place to another, a computer must have an unique address, or *domain name*. In

the language of cyberspace, a domain name is an alphanu-
meric address that can be read by all computers. This cyberspace address allows your computer to connect with other
computers on the Internet. For example, the domain name of
the University of Toronto Faculty of Law is www.law.
utoronto.ca; the domain name for *Wired,* a popular Internet
magazine, is www.wired.com.

Let's not forget that the Internet has become a huge marketplace. Companies wanting to do business on the Internet
hope to use their registered trademarks such as *Pepsi Cola* or
Labatt's Blue as domain names on the Internet. However, many
of these companies have found that their unique trademarks
have already been reserved by other Internet users.

Domain names can be reserved directly through the Internet Network Information Center (InterNIC), a U.S.–based
group of companies that provide worldwide network information services for the Internet. In Canada, a company may
register a ".ca" (which stands for Canada) domain name with
CA*networking, a Canadian Internet domain registry. Inter-
NIC registers the more commonly known ".com" (which
stands for commercial) and ".org" (which stands for organization) designations.

Registration of domain names is done on a first come, first
served basis. Hence the problem. Anyone can register a
domain name on the Internet that someone else may have an
exclusive legal right to use outside of the Internet. Why
doesn't this right extend to the Internet? Because the law has
simply not caught up with the Internet yet. When I started
writing this book, it was possible for anyone to register a
domain name even if that name was in regular use as a
registered trademark by someone else. However, in the last
year, as we'll discuss below, InterNIC has changed its
policy on domain name registration because of some well-
publicized disputes over domain names. InterNIC now

requires that the applicant certify that he or she has a bona fide right to use the requested domain name.

An organization can only register one .ca domain, therefore you should carefully choose the name that best represents your corporation. There is an exception, however. If your organization has both an English form and a French form, you may apply for a .ca domain corresponding to each form.

d.   MORE DOMAIN NAMES ON THE WAY

By far, the most popular domain name extension is the .com name which denotes a commercial or business activity. Because of the rapid expansion of the .com extension, many newcomers to the Web find that their desired domain name is already in use. In order to respond to this problem, an International Ad Hoc Committee of the Internet Society (see the Introduction in this book) has come up with a plan to add seven new extensions, namely:

- .firm, for businesses or firms;

- .store, for businesses selling goods;

- .web, for sites offering activities involving the World Wide Web;

- .arts, for sites emphasizing cultural and entertainment activities;

- .rec, for sites emphasizing recreational activities and entertainment;

- .info, for sites offering information services; and

- .nom, for sites supported by individuals, ie., personal Web pages.

These additional domain names are expected to become available sometime in 1999.

e. DOMAIN NAME DISPUTES

As a result of the recent commercial interest in the Internet, disputes between the rights of trademark owners and domain name owners have surfaced. An example is where one person registers a domain name that someone else already regularly uses as a trade name or trademark to prevent the regular owner from establishing a Web presence or, more likely, to force the legitimate trademark owner to pay a sum of money to acquire the domain name. Some people refer to this sum of money as a ransom.

Many cases have likely been settled out of court through a payment of money. For example, in 1994, Joshua Quittner registered "Mcdonalds.com" as his own domain name. McDonald's Restaurant launched a court action to obtain the name for itself. McDonald's bid was unsuccessful. The case subsequently settled out of court: McDonald's made a charitable contribution in exchange for acquiring the name. Quittner has claimed that his motives in registering the name were more to prove a point than for his own financial gain.

Other cases have been settled in the courts. For example, the use of the name of "MTV.com" has been the subject of litigation. To date, there has been one case decided by the Canadian courts. The case involved a dispute between a Prince Edward Island company and a former employee over the use of the name "PEI.net." The judge found that the use of the name PEI.net was not technically a wrongful use of a trade name, in part because the name was so generic in nature. Although this case does not settle the law completely, it is the only Canadian authority in this area to date.

What, then, can you do to avoid getting embroiled in a domain name dispute? First, register your domain name as soon as possible. You can register a domain name whether or not you have a presence on the Internet yet.

As a result of the rapidly increasing number of disputes over domain names, InterNIC has issued a policy regarding assignment of domain names. As of 1996, InterNIC requires each applicant for a domain name file a statement stating that:

- the applicant has a bona fide right to use the requested domain name;

- the applicant intends to use the name on a regular basis;

- the applicant will not use the name for any unlawful purpose; and

- the applicant's use of the name will not violate any third party's rights in any jurisdiction.

InterNIC now has a dispute resolution procedure if it turns out that someone else has a better right to use of the trademark for which you've applied. If you discover someone else using your trademark, you may file an objection with InterNIC. The other party then has 30 days to prove it has a bona fide right to use the name. If the matter cannot be resolved, InterNIC may suspend the use of the domain name until the matter is resolved by court order or agreement.

The applicant must also agree to defend and indemnify (pay any legal fees) InterNIC for any claims or expense resulting from the wrongful use of the domain name. This policy should reduce the flood of domain name disputes. Before this policy, there was nothing to deter people from registering hundreds of domain names in the hopes of striking the jackpot with the sale of one domain name to the rightful owner of the trademark.

If you are not sure whether someone is using your trademark as a domain name, do an on-line search. InterNIC will inform you if a domain name is available. Just visit the InterNIC home page at rs.internic.net and check out the registration services section.

DOMAIN NAME SPECULATORS BEWARE!

The English Court of Appeal has ruled that the registration of a third party's distinctive name as a domain name will be trademark infringement when such registration is designed to take advantage of the distinctive character and reputation of a trademark in an unfair and detrimental way. Canadian law is based on the English common law system, with the exception of Quebec, and accordingly, a Canadian judge is likely to come to the same conclusion in a similar case.

f.   WHAT HAVE THE COURTS SAID?

Over the past several years the volume of domain name litigation has increased tenfold. While Canadian legal precedent is still relatively scarce, here is a sampling of the types of actions that have been before the American courts:

(a) *Microsoft* versus *Fisher*. This complaint which, at the time of writing, is still unresolved, involves the use of "microsoft.com" and "mnsbc.com" by a defendant for the purpose of misdirecting Internet users to pornographic links. For more information about this case, see www.news.com/News/Item/0,4,35148, 00.html and for information about a similar case involving Paine Webber, an American financial services company, see www.news.com/News/Item/0,4,35259,00.html.

(b) *Avery Dennison Corporation* versus *Sumpton*. This California case involved a Canadian defendant corporation named Free View Listings. Free View was engaged in the business of licensing e-mail addresses from its list of over 12 000 surnames that it had previously registered. One of those surnames belonged to the plaintiff corporation. In this case, a California court decided that Free View would have to relinquish the names to the Plaintiff for a nominal fee of $300 each. The court determined that Free View was liable for trademark infringement because it had registered the names for the sole purpose of keeping others from using them without their consent.

(c) *Toys "R" Us Incorporated* versus *Abir*. In this New York case, Toys "R" Us, owner of the domain name "toys-rus.com" won a preliminary injunction against a cybersquatter's registration and threatened use of the domain name "toysareus.com" in what the court termed a "bad faith effort at cyberpiracy."

At the time of writing this chapter, scores of cases have either been decided by the U.S. courts, settled by the parties involved, or are still pending before the courts. In summary, and based on the cases that have been before the courts so far, a court will most likely prevent the use of a domain name where one or more of the following factors are present:

(a) *The registrant has no legitimate use or entitlement to the domain name.* For example, where the registrant's sole purpose in registering the name is to sell it to someone with a legitimate entitlement to the name. Cybersquatters fall directly into this category and may be defined as an individual or company that registers hundreds or thousands of popular names, phrases, or slogans as domain names for the purpose of later licensing user rights to persons with a commercial need for the domain name.

(b) *The registrant cannot establish a prior use of the registered name.* For example, if a legitimate user can establish use of the disputed name for the past 30 years, an individual that only recently registered the name may be ordered to give it up.

(c) *There is some element of bad faith.* An example of this third category is an actual case involving the owner of a pornographic Web site that was ordered to relinquish the domain name of "nuskin.com" in the face of a complaint by the registered trademark owner, a popular cosmetic manufacturer.

As a final note, it is an unfortunate commentary that many domain names are actually sold by illegitimate registrants, sometimes called cybersquatters. These individuals realize, as do the persons or companies that purchase these domain names, that the costs of protracted and costly trademark litigation sometimes outweighs a payment of hundreds or thousands of dollars to a cybersquatter in order to obtain the rights to use a domain name.

g. PROTECTING YOUR DOMAIN NAME AND OTHER TRADEMARKS

The best way to protect your domain name is to register it as a trademark under the Trademarks Act. As the law evolves toward protecting existing trademark owners such action may not be necessary for someone who has already properly registered a trademark. For example, someone who has already registered a trademark for superglue, probably will have sufficient protection after having obtained the domain name "superglue.com".

In addition to your domain name, which may incorporate your company's trademarked name, your Web page will also display unique features or trademarks. For example, your Web page might include a unique logo or graphic which should be protected. An area that has been the subject of much discussion is whether the actual interface of the Web page (the look and feel of the Web page — how it is set up and presented to visitors) may be protected by either copyright or trademark. Unfortunately this issue has not yet been dealt with by the courts in Canada or, to the author's knowledge, the United States.

Remember that it is just as important to ensure that these unique features are protected as it is to make sure that your Internet address, or domain name, is protected.

h. ENFORCING YOUR TRADEMARK RIGHTS

As the owner of a trademark, you have exclusive use of that trademark. You can give permission to others to use your trademark; such permission is often granted in the form of a licence. For example, if a donut franchiser wants to give permission to its franchisees to use its name, logo, and packaging, it will grant a licence to each franchisee.

Someone who violates your rights by using your trademark without your permission is guilty of trademark infringement. Trademark infringement occurs when someone uses your trademark as their own (or a mark similar or indistinguishable from your mark), or uses your trademark in a way that is likely to confuse others as to the exact source of the goods and services. The trademark does not necessarily need to be identical to constitute infringement. For example, a company attempting to sell computers under the name of "Compact" could be infringing the trademark of Compaq.

The key to establishing trademark infringement is showing that the infringer has used the trademark deliberately to cause confusion as to the source of the goods or of services. If two parties are using identical marks to sell similar goods, the issue becomes one of priority: which party registered the mark first? If neither party registered their trademark, the matter will likely be decided on the basis of who started using the mark first.

The courts will use a number of remedies to stop trademark infringement. One remedy is an injunction — a court order to the infringing party to stop using the trademark. The courts can also award damages for any loss of profits or damage to reputation to the rightful owner of the trademark. Going to court because someone has infringed on your trademark can be complicated and you will likely want to have a lawyer experienced in trademark and intellectual property litigation assist you.

TIPS AND TRAPS

SELECTING A GOOD TRADEMARK

The trademark you choose for your product or service should be distinctive and easily recognized. You must also be careful not to infringe on an existing trademark.

a. WHAT MAKES A STRONG TRADEMARK?

You should consider the following when deciding on your own trademark:

- The most important aspect of a good trademark is its originality. It should be unique and distinct from other companies' trademarks to help your company stand out from the crowd.

- The best kind of trademark is one that is strongly identified with the product it represents. Some trademarks are so successful that people use the trademark name for the generic product: Kleenex and Walkman are good examples of such trademarks.

- The trademark should also convey the impression you want other people to have of your business — the style or image that you want your company to project.

Remember, if your trademark is truly unique, it is very unlikely that it is already being used by someone else. Trademarks do not necessarily have to involve words, for example, they can be graphic-based, as logos are.

If you are unable to come up with a satisfactory trademark for your product, you might want to look into hiring an advertising agency. Advertising agencies will come up with a name for your product and will design the total presentation of the name — the design and style of the type as well as graphic elements or logos.

b. AVOIDING TRADEMARK INFRINGEMENT

Before you go to the expense of putting your trademark on your Web page, make sure no one else is using it first. Do a thorough search on the World Wide Web. By using a search engine such as Yahoo! or Webcrawler, you will get a good idea of whether or not someone else is already using your trademark. If, after doing your on-line search, you find that no one is using your trademark, you should then conduct a trademark availability search. A lawyer will be able to do this search for you. If the lawyer discovers trademarks that are not identical but similar, he or she can give you an opinion as to whether or not your use of the trademark will violate the similar trademarks.

7

PROTECTING TRADE SECRETS ON-LINE

a. WHAT IS A TRADE SECRET?

There is no magic to the term trade secret. A trade secret is simply any information that is confidential and has economic value. For example, your company's customer list, secret recipe, or marketing plan can all be considered trade secrets. Even the smallest business operation can have many trade secrets worthy of protection.

Disclosure of trade secrets is often a necessary part of normal business operations. Your employees need access to certain information in order to function within their jobs. The same is true of consultants you deal with and, in some cases, customers. The computer network in a law firm, for example, is subject to access by a whole host of persons such as lawyers, employees, and third parties such as hardware and software suppliers and consultants. Such information is protected as a trade secret so long as disclosure is made in confidence — that is, under circumstances that legally obligate the recipient to keep the secret.

Establishing a confidential relationship with everyone who will have access to your confidential information is critical. The law prohibits someone with access to a trade secret from using or disclosing the trade secret without the consent of the owner. If that person discloses information which he or she knows to be a trade secret, he or she is in violation of a confidential relationship.

This means that there needs to be more than the disclosure of a trade secret without the consent of the owner: there must also be an understanding, either explicit or implicit, that the material was to be kept confidential. Preferably this understanding will be set out in writing, in advance, in the form of a confidentiality agreement.

While the law pertaining to trade secrets can be somewhat complicated and sometimes involve other issues such as copyright, theft, and fraud, in general, a disclosure of secret information is confidential and subject to protection from disclosure when:

(a) the person to whom the secret is disclosed explicitly promises to keep it secret. A good example of this is where the person signs a non-disclosure or confidentiality agreement before the secret information is provided to him or her; or

(b) the secret information is disclosed in the context of a relationship in which the law will imply an obligation of confidentiality. One of the best examples of an implied obligation of confidentiality is an employee-employer relationship. The law is clear that a senior or managerial employee of a company cannot use secret information for his or her personal benefit. If someone stands in a position of authority over another person, that person is said to have a *fiduciary obligation* to the person over whom he or she has control. A fiduciary duty exists where one party places special trust or confidence in another party. A prime example is the obligation owed by a lawyer to a client: the client relies on the good faith of the lawyer in transacting business. The duty can be explicit or implied. In some relationships, the existence of a fiduciary obligation is obvious, for example, in relationships between a lawyer and client or a doctor and patient. In other cases the existence of the fiduciary duty may be less clear.

b. KEEPING TRADE SECRETS CONFIDENTIAL

The key to protecting your trade secrets is to make sure that the recipient of the information is notified that the disclosed information is a valuable trade secret. Remember that confidential information is confidential only if it is conveyed in circumstances where it is clear that the information must not be disclosed.

When secret information is conveyed to someone outside the employment relationship, it is absolutely necessary that a non-disclosure agreement be signed by the parties. It is important to remember that the non-disclosure agreement must be signed before the secret information is conveyed. If you are dealing with someone on-line, a standard written confidentiality agreement must be in place before the communication takes place.

Alternatively, the confidential relationship may be established through the use of an on-line confidentiality agreement, like the one discussed below. There is no difference

between the written confidentiality agreement and an on-line agreement, except in the way it is transmitted. If the written agreement is to be used on-line, it would be wise to have the parties exchange a message confirming their mutual intention to be bound by the agreement (because of the inability to transmit signatures on-line), for example: I have read the Confidentiality Agreement dated _____.
I enter into this agreement voluntarily and intend to be bound by its terms.

See *Protecting Trade Secrets*, another book in the Self-Counsel Series, for a complete discussion of this issue.

c. HOW DO TRADE SECRETS LOSE THEIR PROTECTION UNDER THE LAW?

Unrestricted disclosure of secret information will result in the loss of its protection, for example, when a person fails to take the necessary precautions to ensure that a relationship of confidentiality is created before the information is conveyed.

Alternatively, the confidentiality aspect of information may be lost when it is posted to the Internet on an unrestricted basis by the owner of that information. A California court dealt with this exact scenario and commented:

> One of the Internet's virtues — that it gives even the poorest individuals the power to publish to millions of readers — can also be a detriment to the value of intellectual property rights. The anonymous (or judgment proof) defendant can permanently destroy valuable trade secrets, leaving no one to hold liable for the misappropriation. Although a work posted to an Internet news group remains accessible to the public for only a limited amount of time, once that trade secret has been released into the public domain, there is no retrieving it.

Sending secret information over the Internet, then, raises a number of a security risks. Whether or not you will want to send secret information over the Internet depends, of course, on the situation. Obviously, transmitting a highly confidential and costly patent application electronically is probably not a wise idea. In some cases, however, attaching the words private and confidential to a communication may be sufficient to protect its confidentiality. Security measures such as encryption are another option.

d. TRADE SECRET LEGISLATION

Often, trade secrets are discussed in the same context as copyright and other intellectual property rights. Although trade secret rights are not as universally recognized and protected as copyright, they are recognized by most countries. The North American Free Trade Agreement, for example, obliges member countries (currently the United States, Canada, and Mexico) to protect trade secrets from unauthorized acquisition, disclosure, or use. Similarly, the General Agreement on Tariffs and Trade (GATT), of which Canada is a signatory party, obliges member countries to protect "undisclosed information" that has commercial value and that is not available to the general public.

e. CONFIDENTIALITY AND NON-DISCLOSURE AGREEMENTS

A non-disclosure agreement is useful when outsiders need access to your organization's confidential data, whether as a basis for evaluation related to the purchase of your company, or for an assessment of your computer system. Using a non-disclosure agreement will help protect your trade secrets, as the receiving party is acknowledging that general disclosure of your information is not permitted.

Sample #2
CONFIDENTIALITY AND NON-DISCLOSURE AGREEMENT

THIS AGREEMENT is made between_____

_____and

_____

(the "parties") and is entered into this ____ day of _____, 200-
in the city of _____.

This Agreement is based on the following mutual understandings:

(a) the parties wish to disclose information, generally, for the purpose of conducting business together;

(b) each party wishes to protect the information which may be disclosed to the other during their business relationship; and

(c) each party enters into this Agreement voluntarily and intends to be legally bound by it.

IN CONSIDERATION of the mutual promises and undertakings in this Agreement, the parties agree as follows:

1. DEFINITION OF CONFIDENTIAL INFORMATION

For the purposes of this Agreement, Confidential Information will refer to all information that is exchanged by the parties during their business relationship. Without limiting the generality of this definition, Confidential Information will include business plans, financial information, pricing information, and all information concerning "Product X."

2. NONDISCLOSURE OF CONFIDENTIAL INFORMATION

Each party will disclose Confidential Information to the other during their business relationship. Neither party will disclose Confidential Information to any person other than persons employed by the parties having a business need for the Confidential Information.

In order to ensure that the Confidential Information is not disclosed to the public, the parties agree:

(a) upon the request of one party, the other will immediately return all tangible material containing Confidential Information including all copies, notes, diskettes, etc. Neither party will retain any confidential

Sample #2 — Continued

information in a computerized storage medium after having been asked to return it to the other party;

(b) to take reasonable precautions to protect the secrecy of the Confidential Information.

3. OWNERSHIP OF CONFIDENTIAL INFORMATION

Both parties acknowledge that they each retain ownership of their Confidential Information despite having disclosed it in accordance with this Agreement. In addition, the parties agree that this Agreement will not be construed as a transfer or licence regarding the Confidential Information.

4. TERM OF THIS AGREEMENT

This Agreement will continue in force until the parties agree, in writing, that the Confidential Information is no longer confidential.

5. REMEDIES UPON BREACH OF THIS AGREEMENT

If one party breaches this Agreement (or threatens a breach), the parties agree that the harm suffered by the aggrieved party will not be compensated by monetary damages alone. The aggrieved party will be entitled to an injunction in addition to any other remedies that might be available to remedy the breach.

6. BINDING ON ALL PARTIES

This Agreement will be binding and enforceable upon the parties, their successors, and assigns.

IN WITNESS WHEREOF, the parties have signed this Agreement which shall take effect on the above date.

_____   _____

Signature   Signature

This type of agreement is not limited to situations in which you are dealing with outside parties. Many organizations require their own employees to sign such agreements to avoid a situation where an ex-employee uses your confidential information against you.

The most important part of the agreement is setting out what information is to be considered confidential and what information is not. Sample #2 shows a typical confidentiality agreement which can be used where both parties wish to protect their information. If you intend to adopt this agreement for your own use, keep in mind that it is a basic agreement and does not contain the more complex terms and provisions that might be present in a broader agreement. If your situation is complicated, you should see a lawyer.

TIPS AND TRAPS

WHAT TO DO IF SOMEONE USES YOUR CONFIDENTIAL INFORMATION

When trade secrets are wrongfully disclosed or confidential information misused, the remedies available are very similar to those for breach of copyright.

1. The offender can be sued, however you must be able to show that you have suffered some kind of harm from the disclosure. Usually the harm is based on loss of profits. An example of this is where the breach of confidential information allows a competitor to market a similar product, resulting in a loss of business for a company due to the increased competition.

2. In an employment situation, misuse of confidential information could form the basis of a dismissal. Employers should be careful, however, as the misuse of information must be serious in order for there to be grounds for dismissal.

3. The court may grant an injunction to prohibit the disclosure. If the court is unwilling to grant an injunction — because the injunction would cause undue hardship to one party — the court can order an accounting of profits resulting from the use of the confidential information.

4. In some cases the wrongful use of confidential or private information, such as a name or photograph, can form the basis on a civil lawsuit on the grounds of breach of privacy. The Privacy Act in British Columbia, for example, specifically makes the wrongful use of another person's name or portrait in order to promote a product an actionable wrong. In this case, wrongful use means without permission.

5. The Internet is obviously a worldwide endeavour. While in Canada the law relating to trade secrets is based on the common law, other countries (such as the United States) have specific trade secrets legislation. If a jurisdiction outside of Canada is involved, specific trade secret legislation, which will likely contain penalties for trade secret infringement, may apply.

8
PRIVACY RIGHTS

a. WHAT IS PRIVACY?

The right of privacy has taken on new meaning in the computer age because of the highly sophisticated technology which has become a part of our daily lives. Today, most of the information about who we are and what we have done is stored on computers. Consider the following examples of highly sensitive information that individuals would not want disclosed without their knowledge and consent:

- Arrest records
- Bank records
- Medical records
- Employment records
- Tax records

- School records

This is only a sample of the kind of personal information available on computerized data banks. As more and more personal information is being stored on computerized databases, the possibility for misuse of such information and unlawful intrusion into these databanks becomes an ever greater threat.

Generally, the law recognizes the right of an individual to simply be left alone. There are many provincial laws setting out specific protection for certain kinds of records. These laws make it illegal to release a confidential record about someone without that person's prior consent. For example, it is unlawful for employers to obtain hospital records for prospective employees to determine whether they have pre-existing medical conditions.

The right of privacy, however, is a concept that is used in a variety of ways to refer to different things. Often it is misunderstood. It is important to remember that some aspects of privacy are protected by law while others are not.

The following aspects of an individual's right of privacy are important in the context of the storage of electronic information:

- *Privacy of identity.* People have a right to be who they are. The misappropriation of a person's name, identity, and other essential characteristics can be a civil wrong and an offender may be ordered to pay damages. At the same time, the misappropriation of a person's personality could be the subject of criminal action.

- *Privacy of data.* Persons have a right to confidentiality of essential data about them. The unauthorized release of records such as social insurance numbers, credit card numbers, medical history, and political affiliations could give rise to liability for damages.

• *Privacy of communications.* There is also, in some cases, a right to privacy of on-line communications. The widespread usage of e-mail has made this issue quite controversial. It is now recognized that in certain circumstances, monitoring or disclosing the contents of electronic communications by anyone other than the sender or the attended recipient can constitute an invasion of privacy.

1. Is your right to privacy threatened by a "cookie"?

A "cookie" is a small chunk of data that is sent to your computer from a particular Web site that you may choose to visit. The cookie's mission is to collect information about your particular visit to that Web site. If, for example, you click on an advertisement for golf clubs, the cookie will remember that you are interested in golf and tailor the information that you receive the next time that you visit the site. Advertisers obviously love cookies because they allow them to tailor the particular advertising that you may receive. The question is, though, are cookies a threat to your privacy?

The answer is, probably not. Cookies don't really contain any personal information about you, because a cookie can only be read by the Web site that installed it in the first place. This could change, however, once companies figure out a way to link cookies to a file of your personal information. Unfortunately, so many Web sites now use cookies that they are viewed by many as a nuisance because every new visit to a Web site starts with a polite, but sometimes annoying, request to install a cookie.

Should you install a cookie on your Web site? First consider whether it is really necessary. Some people get so annoyed by cookies that they simply will move on to another site if they encounter one. Many people go one step further and set their Web site browsers to warn of incoming cookies so that they can be avoided.

2.   Privacy legislation

In the United States, the right of privacy is enshrined in the First Amendment of the United States' Constitution. In Canada, on the other hand, there is no comprehensive right of privacy recognized in the Canadian Charter of Rights or elsewhere. The federal government has a Privacy Act which applies to the release of personal information held by the government. Under the Privacy Act, no information about a person can be released by a government department until the person concerned has been notified and given the chance to object. This act does not apply to private corporations or individuals.

On October 1, 1998, the Personal Information and Electronic Documents Act ("the bill") was introduced in federal parliament. At the time of writing this chapter, the bill has not yet become law. Nonetheless, this new law has wide-sweeping implications for all private business and especially those engaged in e-commerce. This law is certainly "required reading" for all private businesess involved with the Internet and is available at the Government of Canada Web site located at www.parl.gc.ca.

The bill sets standards for the use of digital signatures and sets other benchmarks for the use of electronic information in government and business. The bill also incorporates the ten principles set out in the Canadian Standard Association's Model Code for Protection of Personal Information which are discussed in detail in this chapter. Highlights of the privacy aspects of this bill include:

(a) The bill defines "personal information" as information about an identifiable individual that is recorded in any form.

(b) Organizations must provide complaint procedures and investigate all complaints regarding a failure to comply with the provisions of the bill.

(c) Businesses must ensure that the information they collect is accurate and must employ safeguards to prevent the unauthorized disclosure of information. As a result, businesses that allow visitors to post information to a Web site should employ extreme care to make sure that information is safeguarded and used only for purposes authorized by the giver of the information.

(d) In all cases, consent should be obtained from the individual providing the information and, in addition, companies must permit an individual with the means to access his or her own personal information for the purpose of verifying its accuracy or challenging compliance with the legislation.

There are also a number of provincial acts, such as Ontario's Freedom of Information Act, which operate in a similar way to the Privacy Act. Within the Criminal Code, there are prohibitions on the interception and taping of private communications, including cellular or telephone messages.

In Europe, privacy rights and the safeguarding of information about individuals have received much broader protection than in Canada. In July 1995, the European Union Council adopted a directive on the protection of personal data which deals with both the processing of personal data and the freedom of this data. The policy is widely referred to as the European Privacy Directive. The directive came into force on January 1, 1998.

The provisions of the directive are broad and encompass virtually any information about an identifiable individual. The directive regulates all forms of processing of personal data, including collecting, recording, storing, adapting, retrieving, making available, or destroying data.

Persons who collect and maintain personal data must abide by four key areas of responsibility. They must ensure that:

(a) personal data is processed fairly and lawfully;

(b) personal data is collected and processed only for a specific and legitimate purpose;

(c) personal data is accurate and up-to-date; and

(d) personal data is kept no longer than necessary for the purpose for which it was collected.

Of primary importance is the notion of processing data lawfully, which means that it is necessary for a legitimate purpose and that the person supplying the data has consented. The directive also defines sensitive data as that which relates to racial or ethnic origin, political opinion, religious or philosophical beliefs, trade union membership, health information, or sexually related information.

3.   Quebec Civil Code

Quebec has been at the forefront of championing privacy rights in North America. Quebec, for example, was the first North American jurisdiction to adopt privacy legislation that applies to the private sector. The Quebec Civil Code contains a number of provisions regarding privacy that apply to data on computers and in cyberspace. For example, Article 35 of the code provides, "Every person has a right to the respect of his or her reputation and privacy."

Article 36 of the code also defines a number of specific acts as "invasions of privacy of a person," such as:

- intentionally intercepting or using his or her private communications;

- appropriating or using his or her image or voice while he or she is in private premises;

- keeping his or her private life under observation by any means;

- using his or her name, image, likeness, or voice for a purpose other than the legitimate information of the public; and

- using his or her correspondence, manuscripts, or other personal documents.

The code also sets out a procedure for legally gathering personal information and the making of files concerning other people. The most important aspect of the code is a requirement that no one may invade the privacy of a person without the consent of the person.

4. Model Code for the Protection of Personal Information

The Canadian Standards Association (CSA) has also taken steps toward implementing a code regarding the collection of personal information. The CSA is a federal organization with responsibility for passing standards for many of the products we use in our everyday lives (you can see a CSA approval stamp on most consumer products that you purchase). The CSA has released a final draft Model Code for the Protection of Personal Information (the CSA Code). The CSA Code has been adopted and implemented by the Standards Council of Canada and is now in force. These are some of the basic principles of the draft CSA Code:

(a) *Accountability.* An organization must designate a person who will be responsible for the integrity of confidential information.

(b) *Identifying purposes.* The purpose for which private information is sought should be disclosed at the time it is collected.

(c) *Consent.* Consent should be obtained before private information is collected.

(d) *Limiting collection.* The collection of private information should be limited to legitimate purposes. In other words, fishing expeditions should be discouraged.

(e) *Limiting use, disclosure, and retention.* Except with consent of the person from whom it was obtained, personal information should be used only for the purpose for which it was originally obtained.

(f) *Accuracy.* Personal information should be accurate, complete, and up-to-date.

(g) *Safeguards.* Private records must be protected by some sort of security system.

(h) *Openness.* Policies dealing with confidential record management should be made readily available.

(i) *Individual access.* Persons should be able to access their personal records and challenge their accuracy.

(j) *Challenging compliance.* A dispute resolution process should be made available to persons wishing to challenge compliance with the foregoing principles.

Except with the consent of the person from whom it was obtained, personal information should only be used for the purpose for which it was originally compiled.

Another organization that has done a great deal of work in the area of privacy rights and on-line communication is Electronic Frontier Canada (EFC). EFC was founded to ensure that the principles embodied in the Canadian Charter of Rights and Freedoms are protected as new computing, communications, and technologies emerge.

EFC itself has formulated a number of policies dealing with Canada's computing and communications infrastructure. EFC's Web site is a must-see if you are interested in learning more information about this subject. The EFC Web site can be found at insight.mcmaster.ca/org/efc/.

b. PRIVACY OF E-MAIL COMMUNICATIONS

Today many of us use e-mail to conduct business at our workplace. Every organization with an e-mail system should consider a number of significant issues, including:

- Does monitoring of employee e-mail violate an employee's privacy rights and expose the employer to liability?

- Can an employer be liable for an employee's use of the company's e-mail system to defame, harass, or engage in other offensive communication?

- Can an employer be liable when an employee uses an e-mail system to infringe on another person's copyright or to receive or send obscene material or child pornography?

- Who owns the materials created on an e-mail system?

- Should employees be allowed to use the e-mail system to exchange private or personal communications that are not part of the company's business?

- What can be done to prevent an employee from harassing another employee by sending messages that contain offensive statements?

E-mail provides an ideal medium in which to harass others in the workplace. This capacity combined with the ability to maintain anonymity in such communications may encourage people to act in ways that they might not otherwise. The use of e-mail to harass another employee could constitute discrimination under human rights legislation enacted by the various provinces and expose an employer to possible harassment claims.

INTRANET

An Intranet is essentially a small and private version of the Internet contained within a given company. Large corporations and organizations often have such computer systems for internal communications.

Every company should clearly spell out what is allowed and what is not allowed in terms of proper use of the company's e-mail system. Knowing what is and what is not permitted at the outset can help avoid an embarrassing or troubling situation later. Often employees mistakenly believe that their computer files and communications are protected because they have a unique password. This is most often not the case. Many companies retain a copy of all passwords that employees use and, in many cases, the network supervisor will have access to the passwords.

To date, there have been few disputes concerning the proper use of a corporate computer network and e-mail systems. The cases that have arisen so far have been in the United States, mostly in California. Consider, for example, a California case where a number of employees were fired for sending e-mail messages containing inappropriate jokes and messages.

In Canada, an employer is entitled to terminate an employee for just cause — in other words, for good reason. One could well imagine a case where the unauthorized use of an e-mail system could constitute just cause.

The relative lack of cases dealing with improper use of e-mail in the workplace is likely only a temporary condition. We must remember that it has only been within the last few years that companies have connected their computer networks and e-mail systems to the Internet. Until recently, most corporate computer networks were private and were used primarily for intra-organizational information storage and communication. An Internet connection permits employees to send e-mail messages to the outside world. It is more than likely that cases involving use of company e-mail will soon be brought before the courts.

SOME SIMPLE RULES OF THUMB

In most cases, legal rules are simply applications of common sense. Here are some common sense tips for using e-mail in the workplace:

- If you are sending a private and confidential message, label your e-mail accordingly. Most mail software packages permit users to attach security options to e-mails such as "private and confidential" or "for your information only."

- Send a copy of your message to anyone that is mentioned in your communication. After all, if you can't say something to somebody else directly, then perhaps you might want to reconsider saying something at all.

- Keep copies of your e-mail, either in archive or as hard copy, just as you would keep copies of other pieces of correspondence.

c. TECHNOLOGICAL SOLUTIONS

It is unlikely that privacy issues on the Web will be resolved through the passage of laws alone. Technological solutions already play a major role in privacy management on the Internet and are likely to continue to play a role along with privacy legislation. For example, users may now set their browsers to reject cookies, use encryption to scramble their communications, or even send their e-mail through an anonymous remailer to keep their identity confidential. One service even combines numerous privacy protection measures in routing messages through a series of servers that replace the user's address, geographical location, and e-mail address with a pseudonym. For more information about this service, see Freedom Internet Identity Management System, Zeroknowledge at www.zks.net.

d. IMPLEMENTING A POLICY ON E-MAIL USE

The best way to avoid problems, from both the employer's and employee's perspective, is a written policy on e-mail usage. Although use of e-mail systems is wide spread, very few companies have e-mail policies. One estimate made by a large international law firm is that fewer than 10% of companies have e-mail policies on privacy and security, despite the fact that it is very risky for companies and institutions to wait until they have problems before formulating such a policy.

NEED SOME HELP?

If you are having difficulty putting together an e-mail policy for your company, check out www.truste.org. This Web site features a "wizard" to help you automatically generate your own e-mail policy for your Web site.

Creating and distributing a policy statement on e-mail use can reduce the risk of disputes arising between employees and employers. A written policy can also limit a company's liability to third parties for copyright infringement, defamation and other possible e-mail–related claims by shifting liability to the employee. If a well-drafted policy is circulated to employees, it will not be possible for an employee in breach of the policy to say "I didn't know." In addition, the policy could limit the company's exposure to third party claims as in the case of your employee slandering someone outside the company with an e-mail message. You can protect yourself in that situation with a policy that makes it clear that your company does not condone unrestricted personal use of the Internet.

As well as looking at federal and provincial human rights and privacy legislation, employers and employees should also be aware of union rules to determine what employer practices are permitted. For example, labour union rules and statutes may address an employer's refusal to allow employees to use the e-mail system for union activities or to distribute union materials on-line.

You should try to implement a carefully considered e-mail policy that addresses the needs of both the employee and the employer. This policy should be distributed to all employees and enforced uniformly.

You should consider the following issues when writing your e-mail policy:

- *Company property.* It is most important that every e-mail policy statement makes it clear that the company's e-mail system is company property that is to be used for company business.

- *Personal use.* Your policy should state whether e-mail is to be used solely for business purposes, or whether employees will be permitted to use e-mail for personal purposes. Some objective standards will have to be included if the system may be used for personal purposes. For example, using the e-mail system for personal commercial activities is probably not acceptable while sending personal greetings may be.

- *Sexually explicit images or language.* You should include a prohibition against posting e-mail messages containing sexually explicit images or language which may be construed as harassment.

- *Back-up files.* The policy should directly address employees' misconceptions that deleted files will be forever inaccessible. Deleted files are frequently accessible through the company's back-up files.

- *Use of unauthorized passwords.* The e-mail policy should state that the company prohibits unauthorized use of passwords or using another employee's password to gain access to that employee's files.

- *Employer's right to monitor.* In most cases, the employer will want to reserve the right to monitor and obtain the employee's consent to monitor e-mail messages. This right should be included in the policy.

- *Rationale for monitoring.* If the company plans to monitor its employees' e-mail messages, the policy should set out some basis for doing so. Typical reasons for monitoring include job performance, maintenance, auditing, security, or investigative purposes.

- *Confidential information.* The policy should also contain a prohibition against using the e-mail system to send confidential or sensitive information unless the sending of such information is for legitimate business purposes and is approved by management. See chapter 7 for more on confidential information and trade secrets.

- *Encryption of messages.* If confidential or sensitive information is sent via e-mail, the company may wish to protect itself against the inadvertent disclosure of such information by implementing rules for the encryption of certain messages.

- *Record keeping.* The policy could ask that employees keep hard copies of all e-mail transmissions for record-keeping purposes.

- *Discipline for violation.* Procedures should be included in the policy for disciplining employees who willfully or knowingly violate or abuse the company's e-mail policy. The policy should differentiate between different types of violations and establish a procedure for dealing with violations and the penalties involved. This section could include a system of written warnings leading, if necessary, to termination for repeated violations.

- *The legal weight of e-mail messages.* The policy should explicitly state that e-mail messages are considered "documents" in court proceedings, and therefore can be used as evidence in court proceedings. It may be surprising for some employees to learn that the old adage, "Whatever you say can be used against you in the court of law," applies to e-mail as well.

Sample #3 at the end of this chapter shows a sample company e-mail and Internet policy. It is a good idea to distribute a copy of your Internet and e-mail policy to each employee, get it signed by each employee confirming he or she has read it, and keep a signed copy in his or her employee personnel file.

e. INTERNET IN THE WORKPLACE: SOME SAMPLE U.S. CASES

As discussed earlier in this chapter, there are very few Canadian cases involving the use or misuse of Internet and e-mail in the workplace. There have been a number of cases, though, that have run their course through the U.S. courts. While the U.S. laws are different from Canadian laws, the U.S. cases described below give some indication of how Canadian courts might treat similar situations.

1. Employer monitoring of e-mail

In a California case involving Nissan Motor Corporation, the court determined that the employer had a right to monitor employee's e-mail and to terminate employees for sending e-mail of a personal, sexual nature. Wiretap and privacy laws did not, in this case, protect employees from employer monitoring. Given the passage of new privacy legislation in Canada, it is unclear how a Canadian court would deal with a similar situation. What is clear, though, is that an employer is in a far better position to justify monitoring if that employer has a well-drafted e-mail and Internet policy in the workplace. In another case involving Epson America Incorporated, a California court rejected a plaintiff's attempt to proceed with a class action on behalf of 700 employees who had their e-mail read by their employer.

2. Defamation and discrimination in the workplace

One can easily imagine a disgruntled employee sending hateful e-mails about his or her boss. This situation happened to Intel Corporation. In this case, Intel was successful in arguing that the former employee's e-mails to other employees constituted trespass. The Court gave Intel an injunction to prevent the employee from sending additional messages to Intel employees at work. Earlier in the book we discussed the concept of vicarious liability. In short, vicarious liability makes an employer strictly liable for the acts of an employee acting in the scope of his or her employment. Is an employer liable, then, for discriminatory messages posted by employees on the company computer system? The answer may be, yes. In a case involving Morgan Stanley & Company, a number of black employees where granted authority by the court to proceed with an action against their employer for alleged isolation and denial of advancement opportunities after they complained about the internal dissemination of an October 1995 e-mail message containing racist jokes.

3. Termination for just cause

As discussed earlier, an employer wishing to terminate an employee has two options. The first is to terminate for a good and just reason, like stealing. The second option, if just cause does not exist, is to give the employee reasonable notice or wages in lieu thereof. What is or what is not reasonable varies from case to case. The point is, however, that a number of employers have been successful in arguing that misuse of Internet or e-mail within the workplace constitutes just cause. The same result is likely to take place in Canada. For example, a Pennsylvania court found that the Pillsbury company was within its rights to terminate an employee for transmitting "inappropriate and unprofessional" communications over the company's e-mail system.

TIPS AND TRAPS

DRAFTING AN INTERNET USE POLICY

As we already know, e-mail is an extremely efficient means of communication if it is used correctly. Internet in the workplace can also be a diversion for employees and, in the worst case, an obsession. Employers in the United States have successfully terminated employees for just cause because they were spending too much company time on the Internet.

The use of the Internet in the workplace raises a series of issues ranging from defamatory remarks and harassment, to confidentiality and privacy. Some firms restrict absolutely the use of the Internet in the workplace. This is a form of an Internet policy. Those firms that do allow Internet use in the workplace should consider distributing a well-drafted Internet-use policy to its employees.

> The Privacy Commissioner of Canada's Web page comes with a privacy warning that you may want to adapt for your own Web page. The warning reads: "Personal information sent via the Internet can easily be intercepted. We strongly advise against sending messages containing sensitive personal information to this or any Internet address."

Consider the case where an employee imports a file containing a virus that causes serious damage to the computer system of your business. If your company then becomes involved in a legal action as a result of the virus, you do not want your employee to respond that no one told him or her that this could happen. In this type of case, an ounce of prevention is well worth a pound of cure.

In composing your company's e-mail and Internet policy, you should address the following issues:

- *Privilege versus right.* Establish that Internet use for employees is a privilege, not a right, and that inappropriate use will result in the cancellation of the privilege.

- *Vandalism.* Address the issue of vandalism on the Internet. Users should be advised that any malicious attempt to harm or destroy data of another user will result in cancellation of privileges and possible criminal charges.

- *Viruses.* Ensure that information downloaded from the Internet is thoroughly checked for viruses.

- *Off-limit sites.* Put limitations of the kinds of sites that employees can access on company time. The use of the Internet to access Web sites with sexual themes could be very damaging to your company. Consider a situation where an employee downloads a sexually explicit picture which is inadvertently seen by another employee at your firm. That employee finds the material to be extremely offensive and makes a complaint. Whether or not this constitutes harassment is debatable, however, the situation is definitely a sticky one and is best avoided. The most sensible approach is to issue a statement forbidding employees to use corporate resources to access Internet sites with sexual themes.

- *Confidentiality.* Initiate a policy not to send confidential messages via the Internet and communicate the policy clearly to all employees.

- *Non-business messages.* Warn employees not to use the e-mail system for sending trivial or personal messages. Unless specifically prohibited, employees will tend to use the Internet for broadcasting all sorts of messages. For example, employees will send out searches for missing pens, or advertise dates for company picnics, leading to large numbers of trivial e-mail messages accumulating and occupying valuable space within your computer system.

- *Copyright infringement.* Make it clear that employees must not download, copy, or transmit via the company's network the work of a person outside the organization without that person's permission. There is no problem transmitting works created by one employee to other employees. All employees should be aware that there are strict limits on a person's legal ability to copy and transmit works found on the Internet.

- *Netiquette.* Adopt some general rules for netiquette. There is no mystique here: just apply common sense. Direct users to be polite and remind employees not to send defamatory, abusive, or otherwise harassing messages via the computer system.

- *Signing.* Unless an employee signs the e-mail policy, it may be difficult to prove that the employee was aware of its existence. Having an employee sign the policy at the time of hire, and again when the policy is changed, serves as a record of the employee's consent to the provisions of the policy. This may be important, later on, when the employer attempts to justify its monitoring of employees' on-line activities.

Sample #3 shows a typical company e-mail and Internet policy.

Sample #3
E-MAIL AND INTERNET POLICY

E-MAIL AND INTERNET POLICY
OF ABC CORPORATION

Please read this document carefully.

We are pleased to offer e-mail use and Internet access to the employees of ABC Corporation. Such use is for the use of ABC Corporation employees only. The purpose of this policy is to make you aware of your responsibilities regarding Internet and e-mail use. We believe the Internet offers vast resources of information for our employees. With such access, however, comes the availability of material that will not be considered of value to this company. This policy is drafted for the protection of both you and the company. Because a breach of this policy will be considered a serious breach of your employment contract, we urge you to carefully review this policy and ask any questions that you may have.

Internet — terms and conditions

1. Acceptable use

The purpose of Internet access is to assist you with your work. The use of your account must be in support of work on behalf of ABC Corporation. The use must also be consistent with the objectives of ABC Corporation. If you are unsure about whether or not your use is in accordance with the company's objectives, ask your supervisor. The use of the Internet for your own commercial activities is strictly prohibited, as is the use of the Internet for advertising or political lobbying.

Sample #3 — Continued

2. Compliance with laws

Transmission of any material in violation of federal or provincial law is prohibited and will not be tolerated. This includes the downloading and illegal use of copyrighted material, obscene material, or otherwise sexually explicit material.

3. Network Etiquette

You are expected to abide by these general rules of network etiquette:

(a) Never send abusive, sexist, racist, or defamatory messages.

(b) Assume that all the communications and information accessible via the company's network are the private property of the company.

(c) Be aware that your e-mail communications are not guaranteed to be private. There are other employees of this company who have access to all e-mail. Messages relating to illegal activities will be reported to authorities.

(d) Never send strictly confidential messages over the Internet. If you must send something that is confidential over the Internet, get permission from your supervisor first. Once your supervisor has approved the use of e-mail for confidential messages, make sure the following confidentiality notice is attached: "This document is strictly confidential and intended only for the use of_____ unless otherwise indicated."

4. Vandalism and intentional destruction of data

Vandalism and intentional destruction of computerized data is not only a criminal offence punishable by severe sanctions, it is also a serious breach of company policy and will result in your automatic termination. The company considers vandalism to be any malicious attempt to harm or destroy data of another user

Sample #3 — Continued

(either on the Internet or within the company). This includes, but is not limited to the intentional uploading or creation of a computer virus. Further, it is the company's policy that all employees have access to virus detection software which they will use any time information is being downloaded from an outside source.

5. E-mail use

You must abide by the following guidelines in sending electronic mail messages:

(a) Do not send personal e-mail messages via the company's system.

(b) Avoid sending unnecessary or trivial messages through e-mail.

(c) Make hard copies of your e-mail messages including confirmation of receipt of messages that you send to others. These should be kept in a separate file entitled "e-mail messages."

(d) Do not enter into binding contractual commitments on behalf of the company by e-mail. Authorization to enter into a binding contract over the Internet on behalf of the company must first be obtained from your supervisor.

6. Security

Security of the company's computer system is a high priority. If you are suspicious about a security problem on the Internet or relating to the company's internal computer system, you must notify your supervisor. Do not use another employee's account without written permission from that individual. Attempts to log onto the Internet on an unauthorized account will result in disciplinary action.

9

COMPUTER CRIME

As the number of people using the Internet continues to increase, the opportunities for computer crime increase. What is computer crime? It can be a number of things. It can be the unlawful use of a computer system, such as breaking into a confidential database. It can also be the deliberate transmission of a computer virus. Computer crime is definitely not something new. It is merely adapting traditional notions of criminal behaviour to modern technology. After all, fraud is still fraud and offensive material is still offensive, whether or not it is on-line.

a. CANADIAN LEGISLATION

In Canada, criminal conduct is governed by the federal Criminal Code. Although there have been several amendments to the Criminal Code in the last several years dealing specifically with computer technology, it is still important to remember that all the other provisions of the Criminal Code still apply to computer crime. For example, theft of a computer file still constitutes taking something that doesn't belong to you. The difficulty is that the new technology poses practical problems for investigation and proof.

The Criminal Code makes the following acts criminal offences:

(a) *Unauthorized alteration, destruction, or interference with the use of data.* The Criminal Code protects the integrity of data from alteration or destruction and protects a person's right to access and use data to which they are entitled. This includes protection from someone altering or sabotaging data (i.e., by the distribution of viruses) or other modes of destruction or interference with the use of data.

(b) *Unauthorized access to or use of a computer system.* Legislation was enacted to address the problem of "hacking" in which a computer hacker gains access illegally to confidential computer systems.

    It is an offence under the Criminal Code to fraudulently and without "colour of right:"

    (i) obtain directly or indirectly any computer service, and

    (ii) use or cause to be used, directly or indirectly, a computer system with intent to obtain unlawfully a computer service, intercept its functions (including communications), or cause mischief to its data.

COLOUR OF RIGHT

Colour of right means to have the apparent or presumption of authority without necessarily having that actual legal right. For example, someone may think he or she has a legal right to do something when, in fact, he or she does not. In order to be guilty of having done something fraudulently, that offender must have known, at the time, that the act done was against the law.

The problem with the sections of the Criminal Code that deal with these issues (section 342.1(1)(a) and (c)) is that the application is not always clear: an alarm does not always go off when someone illegally accesses a computer system. The application of these sections can often be quite subtle. Consider these examples.

(c) *Unauthorized interception of computer communications.* It is an offence under the Criminal Code to dishonestly and without colour of right intercept a function (including communications) of a computer system. The key to whether or not the interception of a computer communication is a criminal act is if there is consent on the part of both the sender and receiver of the information.

This aspect of the interception of e-mail messages raises some unique issues. Can an employer monitor electronic mail communications? Many employers do. Since the employer owns its computer system, he or she may monitor the functions of the computer system. As an employee, you are using your employer's facilities and therefore cannot assume that your on-line communications are completely confidential.

(d) *Telecommunications fraud.* The Criminal Code provides that a person is guilty of theft if they fraudulently, maliciously, or without colour of right use any telecommunications facility or obtain any telecommunications service.

Telecommunication fraud has become such a fast-growing and prominent crime that it has developed its own name. *Phreaking* is the illicit access to a telephone system to either steal service or to alter the programming of the telephone master switch. In recent years, phreaking has resulted in significant lost revenue for telecommunications companies.

The penalties for computer crime can be severe. Generally, criminal offences are classified as either summary conviction offences (relatively minor offenses resulting in a fine or brief jail sentence), indictable offences, or hybrid offences where the crown attorney has the option of proceeding either by summary conviction or indictment. The direction in which the prosecutor proceeds usually depends on the severity of the offence. The severity of the punishment depends on a number of factors, such as the extent of the damage caused and whether the accused has any previous convictions for similar offences.

b. U.S. LEGISLATION

Although U.S. law is not binding on Canadian courts, U.S. decisions can be very instructive in illustrating how our laws are likely to develop. Because of its sheer size (50 state legislatures and a federal legislature), the United States has generated a great deal more decisions and precedents involving Internet-related cases than Canada has. In instances where Canadian courts and legislatures have not dealt with a particular issue, U.S. cases can be very useful. Further, much of what goes on in cyberspace is on an international scale.

When you do business on-line with someone outside of Canada, you must be mindful of the impact of not only Canadian laws but international laws as well.

Almost every U.S. state has enacted laws prohibiting unauthorized access to a computer, and almost any on-line contact with a computer is considered access. In addition, the federal government has enacted two statutes dealing specifically with computer crime.

First, the Computer Fraud and Abuse Act (CFAA) prohibits unauthorized access to government computers (i.e., data about national defence or foreign relations), financial institution computers, the computer of a credit card issuer (i.e., MasterCard or Visa), and the computer of a consumer reporting agency (to obtain credit information).

In the case of a computer used by government, the CFAA makes unauthorized access alone an offence. Liability for unauthorized access to other computers requires some extra elements such as obtaining information or damaging existing information.

Second, the Electronic Communications Privacy Act (ECPA) prohibits a third party from intercepting or disclosing electronic communications. The ECPA also prohibits unauthorized access to, and disclosure of, stored electronic communications, including voice mail and e-mail. Sanctions under the ECPA can be severe, ranging from prison terms to fines depending on the violation.

Last, in February 1996, the Communications Decency Act (CDA) was signed into law. The essential purpose of the CDA was to prohibit the use of interactive computer services to make "indecent" material available to minors. This law was not passed, however, without controversy. Many feared that the CDA would reduce the Internet to content that is only fit for children while others feared that the stiff fines and potential jail sentences would have a chilling effect on Internet speech.

As it turned out, the CDA was short lived. In the summer of 1997, Janet Reno, the U.S. attorney general, and the American Civil Liberties Union battled over the constitutionality of the CDA in a widely publicized case before the Supreme Court of the United States. The ACLU won. The Supreme Court decided that the CDA was at odds with the right to free speech enshrined in the First Amendment and, accordingly, the CDA was set aside. Since that time, many democratic governments, including the United States and Canada, have struggled to pass legislation that protects children from pornography on the Internet, while at the same time does not infringe upon a citizen's right to communicate freely.

c. TYPES OF COMPUTER CRIME

As discussed above, the instances in which a computer crime is committed may not be crystal clear. Consider the following examples, taken from a mix of Canadian and U.S. cases:

(a) A courthouse clerk uses a computer system for personal reasons to access information about the criminal record of a friend. Is this act a criminal offence?

(b) An employee accidentally deletes or negligently modifies a program while trying to fix a problem. Has he or she committed a crime?

(c) To protect his or her confidentiality, a person sets up an account for Internet services under a pseudonym and false address. Has he or she committed the offence of unauthorized access to a computer system?

(d) A college student releases a program on the Internet designed to randomly explore and compile information. An unfortunate programming error, however, tranforms the program into a voracious computer virus which infects thousands of computers.

Let's look at each situation in more detail. In the first example, the clerk is probably guilty of a criminal offence. A person's state of mind at the time the crime is committed is important. During the course of his or her training, a clerk would have been told that the unauthorized use of the computer system is prohibited and so would have known that it was wrong to use the system for his or her own personal use. In fact, these same circumstances have resulted in successful prosecutions in several U.S. states.

In the second example, the employee who negligently modifies a program is not guilty of a criminal offence. This situation is different, however, from one in which a disgruntled employee, perhaps after being fired, accesses his or her former employer's computer system to destroy data. The employee in this latter instance *intends* to cause damage.

In the third case, it is doubtful whether the person would be found guilty of unauthorized access to a computer system. That is not to say, however, that he or she is not guilty of some other offence. For example, if the reason for use of the pseudonym was to avoid paying for the services, he or she could be found guilty of fraud or perhaps theft.

The last example is taken directly from the case of *United States* versus *Morris*. In that case, Robert Morris, a Cornell graduate student, was successfully prosecuted under the CFAA. His now infamous program is commonly referred to as the Internet "worm."

Morris' original intention was to create a program that would automatically go from one location to another and make revisions to data. Unfortunately, instead of making well-intentioned revisions to data, the worm program got out of control and went from one computer system to another destroying the data on those computer systems.

d. OBSCENITY ON THE INTERNET

Sex sells. No one knows this better than those individuals that sell or otherwise communicate sexually explicit materials on the Internet. The proliferation of sexually explicit materials on the Internet has been incredible. You need only look at the classified pages at the back of any computer magazine to find reference to the many exotic locations on the World Wide Web all seeking to attract visitors, for a price, to their explicit sites.

Both the Internet and private bulletin board systems (BBSs) make sexually explicit images and text available as well as providing forums for discussing sexually explicit topics. These innovations have not gone unnoticed by parents, law enforcement authorities, legislators, and the general public. Debate about the limits as to what may be transmitted by computers over telephone lines has been heated. In the United States, Congress has passed the Communications Decency Act which regulates the content of information that may be transmitted over the Internet.

The legislation, which deals specifically with the Internet and is widely referred to on the Internet, has not been passed without controversy and opposition. Groups opposing the passage of the legislation have begun a blue ribbon campaign against the notion of regulating information on the Internet as they see such regulation as a limit on freedom of expression.

BLUE RIBBON

The blue ribbon is the symbol of freedom of speech chosen by the Electronic Frontier Foundation, a U.S. organization. The blue ribbon symbol or graphic is widely used on many other Web pages — U.S. and international — to indicate support for the campaign against infringements on the right of free speech. You can visit the

Electronic Frontier Foundation home page at www.eff.org
to find out more information about the blue ribbon campaign.

In Canada, indecent communications on the Internet are
dealt with in the Criminal Code. Although the Code does not
define what is indecent or pornographic, it does contain a
sweeping definition of what is obscene. The Criminal Code
states that "any publication a dominant characteristic of which
is the undue exploitation of sex, or of sex and any one or more
of the following subjects, namely, crime, horror, cruelty, and
violence, shall be deemed obscene."

1.   What is pornography?

The distinction between obscenity and pornography is a
difficult one. Although we all have some general idea of what
people will tolerate, it is difficult to define obscenity for the
purpose of imposing criminal sanctions.

The definition of obscenity is tied into what is accepted
in the community as a whole. The general principle is that
if something is generally accepted by a majority of your
neighbours, it is probably not obscene. In a 1992 decision, the
Supreme Court of Canada outlined how the community
tolerance test should be applied:

> The courts must determine as best they can what the
> community would tolerate being exposed to on the
> basis of the harm that may flow from such exposure.
> Harm in this context means that it predisposed per-
> sons to act in an anti-social manner...the stronger the
> inference of a risk of harm, the lesser the likelihood
> of tolerance...

> If the material is not obscene under this framework,
> it does not become so by reason of the person to
> whom it is or may be shown or exposed nor by
> reason of the place or manner in which it is shown...

> The portrayal of sex coupled with violence will always constitute the undue exploitation of sex. Explicit sex which is degrading or dehumanizing may be undue if the risk is substantial. Finally, explicit sex that is not violent and neither degrading nor dehumanizing is generally tolerated in our society and will not qualify as the undue exploitation of sex unless it employs children in its production.

Applying, then, the community tolerance test, if a BBS offers sexually explicit material that "is not violent and neither degrading or dehumanizing," it would not be considered obscene. Going one step further, the depiction of explicit material on that BBS would not be obscene even if children or teenagers could access the material.

What this means for parents is that children can easily access all kinds of pornography on the Internet within a matter of seconds. This is the reality of cyberspace. What can you do about it? Two things. The first is constant supervision. The second is supervision with the aid of technology. Some Internet service providers offer filtering mechanisms that allow you to prevent access to particular topics on the Web.

Recognizing the need for this type of technology, some companies have developed products that can be installed on your home computer. A Vancouver-based company has a product called Net Nanny, for example.

HOW SEX SITES CAPITALIZE ON MISLEADING URLs

There are many ways a child might come into contact with an adults-only Web site. The contact may be purely innocent. For example, if you type "naughty" into a search engine you will come up with a great many hits. Amongst the search results will be a site offering Santa's list of who is naughty and nice. This site will be nestled in with countless other Web sites which are not as tame.

Even worse, some Web sites deliberately attempt to deceive — www.nasa.com was a well publicized example of such deception. This site contained links to adult Web sites in a blatant attempt to catch browsers who inadvertently failed to arrive at their original destination, namely, www.nasa.gov. Another example of this problem is www.disnie.com.

2. The unique problem of child pornography

On August 1, 1993, the Criminal Code was amended to include provisions making child pornography an offence. It defines child pornography as:

(a) a photograph, film, video, or other visual representation, whether or not it was made by electronic or mechanical means;

   (i) that shows a person who is or is depicted as being under the age of 18 years and is engaged in or is depicted as engaging in explicit sexual activity; or

   (ii) the dominant characteristic of which is a depiction, for sexual purposes, of a sexual organ or the anal region of a person under the age of 18 years; or

   (iii) any written material or visual representation that advocates sexual activity with a person under the age of 18 years that would be an offence under this act.

The new amendments to the Criminal Code not only prohibit the production, distribution, and sale of child pornography but also make possession of such material a criminal offence. Although many countries make the production and distribution of child pornography illegal, the possession of such material is not prohibited in all countries, as it is in Canada. In Denmark, Finland, and Sweden, for example, possession of child pornography is legal.

There have been a number of well-publicized cases of on-line child pornography in Canada. For example, a person who uploaded to electronic BBS stories and images considered to be child pornography was successfully prosecuted under the Criminal Code. In this case, the defendant had scanned images of children from store catalogues, electronically altered the digitized images so that the children's clothes appeared to be removed, and then uploaded these images to a BBS.

The penalty for the distribution of child pornography can be severe and includes imprisonment. Again, like other offences under the Criminal Code, the severity of the penalty depends on a number of factors, most notably, the magnitude of the crime and existence of previous convictions.

e. HATE PROPAGANDA

The Internet is a great equalizer in the sense that anyone can make their views known to millions of people simply by posting them on the World Wide Web. This is not necessarily a bad thing, but the downside of this freedom of expression is the possibility of abuse.

We have all heard of cases involving the hard copy distribution of hate propaganda. The case of *R* versus *Zundel*, for example, involved the distribution of documents claiming the Holocaust never occurred. The ease with which information can be disseminated electronically on the Internet makes it easy for someone to reach a wide audience with a hateful message. Is such conduct illegal?

The Criminal Code creates three offences dealing with the distribution of hate propaganda:

(a) *Advocating or promoting genocide.* The words "advocating or promoting" are important. It would seem to imply that only the person actually making the statement will be held responsible and not necessarily those who enable the expression of the statement such as ISPs or mailing list administrators.

MAILING LIST

A list of e-mail addresses used to forward messages (usually related to a specific topic such as law) to groups of people. Some mailing lists are moderated by persons who decide whether or not to send messages to the entire group.

(b) *Inciting hatred.* The second offence is inciting hatred against any identifiable group by communicating statements in any public place where such incitement is likely to lead to a breach of the peace. Like the first offence, communicating would certainly include a message transmitted via the Internet. Again, persons not actually making the statements such as the ISP would not be held liable unless they actually participated in the crime. In terms of on-line communications, though, the phrase "public place" could be problematic. Is the Internet a public place? The issue has not yet been decided by Canadian courts.

(c) *Willful promotion of hatred against an identifiable group.* The last offence is the wilful promotion of hatred against an identifiable group by communicating statements, other than in private conversation. The difference here is that the statements need not be made in a "public place." A hateful message transmitted from one person to another by e-mail would not likely be an offence. If that message was transmitted during an interactive chat section or posted to a mailing list against an identifiable group, then a crime may have been committed.

CHATTING

Chatting is talking to other people on the Internet in real time as opposed to sending e-mail messages.

The term "identifiable group" is important. The distinction here is that the words "I hate everybody" would not constitute an offence. However, the words "all people that believe in X religion should be hated" could be considered an offence because they isolate a particular group.

Federal and provincial human rights legislation also deals with discriminatory practices. Most provincial human rights laws contain powerful remedies to prevent the distribution of hateful propaganda. These sections could be used to shut down a Web page, chat group, or mailing list that might be considered to be conveying discriminatory messages.

f. WHAT TO DO IF YOU DISCOVER ILLEGAL CONTENT ON THE INTERNET

Sooner or later everybody comes across something that may appear to be illegal if they spend enough time on the Internet. Strictly speaking, "sex sites" are not illegal unless they are "obscene" within the somewhat vague definition provided by Canadian law. Other sites, though, such as distributors of child pornography or hate propaganda are more clearly illegal and have no place on the Internet. What can be done if you encounter these sites?

There are two options. The first is simple — do nothing. The second is to take action. Either call the police or simply e-mail the service provider that may be hosting the site. In Canada, you should find that Internet service providers will be responsive to your concerns. In 1996, iStar Internet Incorporated, Canada's largest service provider at the time, voluntarily blocked all access to child pornography Web sites from its server. Subsequently, the Canadian Association of Internet Providers (CAIP) went one step further and created a voluntary Code of Conduct designed to monitor the content of Web sites hosted by members. The CAIP Code of Conduct is reproduced below with permission:

(a) CAIP will cooperate with all government officials, international organizations, and law enforcement authorities seeking to clarify the responsibilities for each of the different functions performed by Internet companies.

(b) CAIP members pledge to comply with all applicable laws.

(c) CAIP members are committed to public education about Internet issues and technology.

(d) Privacy is of fundamental importance to CAIP members who will respect and protect the privacy of their users. Private information will be disclosed to law enforcement authorities only as required by law.

(e) CAIP members will not knowingly host illegal content. CAIP members will share information about illegal content for this purpose.

(f) Although Internet providers are unable to monitor all content, CAIP members will make a reasonable effort to investigate legitimate complaints about alleged illegal content or network abuse, and will take appropriate action.

(g) Prior to taking any action, upon receipt of such complaints, CAIP members will:

   (i) conduct an internal review to determine the nature and location of the content or abuse, and where warranted;

   (ii) consult with legal counsel and/or outside authorities; and/or

   (iii) notify the content provider or abuser of the complaint, with a request for a response within seven days.

g. UNFAIR COMPETITION AND DECEPTIVE TRADE PRACTICES

Unfair competition and deceptive trade practices are very general terms encompassing many forms of illegal activity ranging from false advertising, consumer fraud, false endorsement, and product or trade libel. There are numerous laws in each province and also federal laws that regulate business and trade competition. For example, there is a federal Competition Act, which among other things prohibits collusion amongst competitors to set price or distribute goods. Each province also has its own consumer protection legislation which is designed to protect consumers from rip-offs, scams, and false advertising. The scope of these statutes is well beyond the scope of this book. Suffice it to say that these laws apply as much in the on-line world as they do outside it.

One aspect of this issue that seems to be unique to the on-line world, however, is the use of keywords or hidden text to lure users to a Web site. For the most part, users will access a Web site, at least on the first occasion, with the assistance of a search engine. Simply put, a search engine — there are many different brands available — searches hidden text or "metatags" that have usually been set up by the Web site developer that has created the page. For example, the owner of a Web site offering legal services may include the following hidden text to identify its page to search engines: law, lawsuit, tort, malpractice, injury. A problem arises, however, when that same law firm includes the name of a competitor law firm for the purpose of misdirecting inquiries to its Web site. This form of trademark infringement is nothing more than unfair competition, although a Canadian court has yet to consider this factual circumstance.

A U.S. court did consider similar facts to those set out above in the case of *Instituform Technologies Incorporated* versus *National EnviroTech Group*. In this case, the court awarded an injunction to prevent the defendant, Envirotech, from using a competitor's trademark in its Web site's hidden text in order to divert business through search engines. The message here, then, is that it is most likely a trademark infringement and a breach of Canadian competition laws to include unique names or trademarks belonging to others in the hidden text of your Web page for the purpose of increasing traffic to your site.

h. DEALING WITH COMPUTER CRIME IN YOUR BUSINESS

The best method for dealing with computer crime is to avoid it in the first place. One of the biggest threats to your computerized information in cyberspace is a computer virus. Equally serious, if not more so, is the risk that someone within your business may intentionally damage your computer system.

There are three ways to deal with computer crime. The first is to install preventive measures such as virus detection software which examines all incoming material. You should also do a general assessment of your business's risk of computer crime (e.g., how often are outside resources imported into your network?). This preventive work is the most effective method because it attempts to anticipate problems or threats before they arise.

The second way of dealing with viruses is by detecting them before they do damage to your system. Many viruses are benign; they lie dormant and create damage to your system only at some specified time. There are software programs which can detect such existing viruses and, in some cases, they can be detected without the assistance of software programs simply by using common sense.

The final way of dealing with computer crime is recovery: making sure you are able to deal with the result once disaster strikes. This is the least preferable method and is, like the second method of detection, reactive. This method entails having accurate backup records and proper recovery strategies in place for replacing your information and getting your system up and running again.

Let's look at each of the three strategies in more detail.

1.   Prevention

Generally there are two ways you can prevent computer crime. The first is to properly set up your computer system with the necessary virus detection software. The second is to properly train and monitor your staff. What follows are a number of issues that should be looked at when assessing the vulnerability of your firm to computer crime. Review the list. If you find that you are answering no to most of the questions, you have some serious work to do in protecting your company from computer crime.

- Is your computer system accessible to individuals outside your business? If the answer is yes, is your system protected by a firewall or other security measure to protect on-line access to your system?

FIREWALL

A firewall is a system that lets only certain kinds of messages into a computer network and filters out such garbage as viruses. Chapter 2 discusses firewalls in more detail.

- Is it your company's policy to reprimand or terminate employees and other parties who commit fraud or computer crime against your business?

- Does your business have well-publicized policies on the personal use of its computer equipment and on-line services?

- Does your business distribute guidelines about safe computing including e-mail use and Internet surfing?

- Does your business have a publicized policy which deals with copying, downloading material from the Internet, and software piracy? Chapter 5, on copyright, discusses software piracy in detail.

- Have your employees been properly trained in the use of your application software?

2.   Detection

Several computer programs designed to detect viruses on computer systems are available. However, having a virus detection program is not enough; you must make sure that you constantly update your software. Hackers are always developing new viruses. Reviewing various virus detection software programs is well beyond the scope of this book, however, we can discuss some methods for recognizing symptoms that could be caused by a virus. Remember that there may be other possible causes for these symptoms and the presence of one of them does not necessarily mean your system is infected.

If you discover one or more of the following symptoms in your computer system it is possible that you may have been infected by a virus:

- Your files suddenly grow in size. Viruses add instructions to your system, taking up space on your hard drive.

- Application programs suddenly take much longer to work and execute standard instructions. For example, your spreadsheet program suddenly takes much longer to crunch a series of numbers than it did before.

- The files in some of your directories may have modification dates. For example, one file in your directory for the word-processing software which was installed on January 1, 1997, has been modified on June 1, 1997. This new date could be a sign that your application has been infected.

- Your applications no longer run because of a lack of memory. Some viruses may be designed to reside in your random access memory. If you have not done anything unusual to your system and, suddenly, you have a memory problem, this could be a sign of a virus.

3. Recovery

If you need to recover all your data and you have not planned ahead, you may be in a bit of trouble. Do not panic. The most important thing to do is attempt to isolate the location of the virus and terminate all contact between the infected computer and other computers in your business. If you lost data, though, it may be gone forever unless you had backed up your information. Here are some useful tips that will make recovery easier:

- Back up all your applications and data on a regular and rotating basis so that if a disaster occurs, clean copies of programs will be available.

- Buy a high-quality virus detection and prevention program and keep it active on your system. Make sure the program is updated and that it detects viruses from all sources — for example, information coming in by way of CD ROM, diskette, or over the Internet.

- Do not make untested software or information public. This includes uploading to a bulletin board or a site on the World Wide Web.

- Run virus checking software before doing backups. This will ensure that your backup copies are not tainted.

- File your original master diskettes or CD ROMs in a safe place. Make working copies from the original diskettes and write protect them before putting them into your computer.

- Do not use pirated software. This is a common source of viruses.

Overall, keep a sense of perspective about viruses and the Internet. Instances of viral infection through the Internet are rare. Furthermore, not all viruses are going to destroy all the data on your machine. Viruses should not prevent you from accessing the wealth of information on the Internet.

TIPS AND TRAPS

THE RESPONSIBLE PARENT IN CYBERSPACE

There are many things from which parents must protect their children. In many cases, parents can only do their best to instill values in their children and then they must leave it up to the children to exercise their own judgment. The Internet and World Wide Web offer vast opportunities for accessing information. Much of that information has the potential to expand our children's horizons. Some of that information, unfortunately, will not.

As a parent, the most important thing you can do to teach your children to use the Internet wisely is to simply be aware. Become knowledgeable about the various issues and pitfalls of the Internet and discuss Internet use with your children. Here are some suggested topics of discussion by Matt Carlson, author of *Child Proof Internet: A Parent's Guide to Safe and Secure Online Access:*

- Tell your children that, regardless of who asks, they should never give out their name, address, or telephone number over the Internet.

- As a preventative measure, it is probably a good idea to make sure that your e-mail address is not given out without your permission.

- Your children should understand that many of the general rules that apply in the outside world apply in cyberworld. For example, strangers are strangers whether you meet them on the street or on the Internet. Your children are not going to be able to know with whom they are dealing as on-line interaction is completely anonymous.

- Never allow your child to arrange a personal meeting with another computer user without your permission.

- No personal information about your family, such as photographs of you and your family members or credit card numbers, should be given out over the Internet.

- If you become aware of any child pornography on the Internet, you should immediately call the police and your ISP.

- Encourage your children to participate in bulletin boards and chat groups that are monitored. Unmoderated chat groups typically contain a lot of garbage. On the other hand, moderated groups usually have an administrator who filters out extraneous and vulgar material from the service.

- Establish limits for the number of hours per day and per week your children can be on-line. Carlson suggests using a calendar chart that sets out the number of hours on a daily, weekly, and monthly basis. There is also a practical reason for setting such limits. If you are using your home telephone line to access the Internet, you will not be able to use your telephone while family members are on-line.

- Talk to your children about the expense of Internet access. Teach them to use the Internet wisely by downloading mail and reading it off-line. If more than one child requires Internet access, you will need to work out a way to share Internet access that fits your budget.

A copy of a sample parenting agreement for safe surfing can be found at Carlson's home page www.safesurfing.com.

In his book, Carlson invites readers to copy the following contract onto their word processor and amend it to reflect their own needs. Remember that you are dealing with children or teenagers, so make your Internet agreement as easy to read as possible. It should not look like a legal document. Carlson also suggests posting it in a conspicuous place near your computer work area in the home. The contract is reproduced below with permission:

OFFICIAL INTERNET CONTRACT

I,_____, agree to abide by the following rules that are necessary for my safe use and enjoyment of the Internet:

- I will not surf the Internet for more than _____ hours per day, _____ hours per week, or _____ hours per month.
- I will keep my parents informed of all my activities on the Internet at all times.

- I will never give out personal information — including my telephone number, address, or the name or location of my school.

- I will avoid unpleasant situations. If I find myself in such a situation, I will log off the Internet and report it to my parents.

- I will always be myself.

- I will stick to my budget.

- I will always express myself in a cool and calm manner.

- I will treat others as I would want to be treated myself.

- I will help newbies if they are having problems surfing the Internet.

- I will always use my common sense.

- I will treat everyone on the Internet with respect.

- I will share good ideas or information that I have.

- I will be an active and useful member of cyberspace.

- I will inform my parents if I come across any information that makes me feel uncomfortable or weird.

- I will never agree to get together with someone I "meet" on the Internet without my parents' permission. If I get their permission, my parents will come with me and the meeting will take place in a public place.

- I will not visit areas on the Internet that are off limits to me.

If I do not follow these rules and guidelines, I realize that my Internet or other privileges will be taken away and I will not be able to surf the Internet for a period of ____ days/____hours.

Dated:_____

_____

Signature of child

_____

Signature of parent

10

LEGAL RESEARCH ON THE INTERNET

There is a lot of useful legal information on the Internet. The trick is knowing how to access it. This is especially true as the amount of legal information on the Internet is increasing at an exponential rate. Within the next several years, it is quite likely that everything you need will be on the Internet.

You can access information on the Internet in one of three ways. First, you may visit the Web site of an organization, governmental body, business (e.g., a law firm), or educational facility. Some of these Web sites contain incredible amounts of information and will lead you to other interesting sites on the World Wide Web.

You can also subscribe to a mailing list which will allow you to have regular access to information and documentation on specific subjects of interest to you.

The third avenue is to join a newsgroup or discussion group. Participation in a newsgroup or discussion group will allow you to discuss legal topics of interest with others who have similar interests.

a. WHAT'S OUT THERE? INTERESTING LEGAL WEB SITES

The World Wide Web is exactly what it sounds like. It is a web-like computer system spanning thousands of computers all over the world that has two important characteristics. First, the Web allows for interactive media, meaning it allows access to all forms of media including documents, video, photographs, sound recordings, and graphics. The second important component of the Web is its links. Links are electronic pointers that take people from one place to another on the Web, allowing them to surf the Internet. For example, if you are doing legal research from your computer in New Zealand, you can go directly into a government computer in Ottawa to check the wording of a statute. All of this can be done via the Internet in the span of two minutes.

What is on the World Wide Web for you? Because it is global, the Web represents a new and revolutionary way to access information from all around the world. With your home computer linked to the Internet, you suddenly have a gigantic library available to you in your own living room. You will be able to access almost anything you might need to know about the law of the Internet. You can get copies of statutes and find articles written by law professors and law students. You will also be able to find copies of court decisions and sample legal forms ranging from non-disclosure agreements and Web site development agreements to Internet use policies. Because of the speed at which the Internet is growing — and changing — some Web addresses may no longer be valid when you try to access them. If this happens, use a search engine to try to locate the site.

1.   Government Web sites

The federal and provincial parliaments have their own Web sites and each offers access to government publications and legislation. Here are the addresses:

Federal parliament: www.parl.gc.ca

Alberta: www.assembly.ab.ca

British Columbia: www.gov.bc.ca

Manitoba: www.gov.mb.ca/leg-asmb/index.html

New Brunswick: www.gov.nb.ca/legis/index.htm

Newfoundland: www.gov.nf.ca/house

Northwest Territories: www.assembly.gov.nt.ca

Nova Scotia:www.gov.ns.ca/legi/index.htm

Nunavut: www.nunavut.com

Ontario: www.ontla.on.ca

Prince Edward Island: www.gov.pa.ca/leg

Quebec: www.assnat.qc.ca

Saskatchewan: www.legassembly.sk.ca

Yukon: www.gov.yk.ca/legassem.html

2.   Courts on the World Wide Web

Many of the decisions made by Canadian courts are now available through the Internet. You may find some cases related to cyberspace here, as well as decisions on various other cases. Here are some interesting starting points:

(a) The Supreme Court of Canada's Web page has more than just a nice colour photograph of the front of the Supreme Court of Canada building located in Ottawa. It also contains information about each of the Supreme Court Justices and allows you to access recent rulings from the Supreme Court. The page is available in either French or English and is located at: www.scc-csc.gc.ca.

(b) The Federal Court has jurisdiction over matters that are national in scope, such as tax, immigration, defence, and admiralty. You may access full text decisions of the Federal Court by visiting: www.fja-cmf.gc.ca/en/cf/index.html.

(c) The House of Lords is the highest court in the United Kingdom. Although the decisions made by the House of Lords are not technically binding on our courts, the reasoning of the House of Lords' decisions are often adopted by our own courts and are considered to be persuasive because we share the same common law legal system. The House of Lords' home page may be found at: www.parliament.the-stationery-office. co.uk/pa/ld/ldhome.htm.

3.   U.S. legal information

You will find a vast amount of legal information and advice on the Internet, much of it from U.S. Web sites. While this information can be interesting and instructive, don't assume that the same rules apply in Canada.

United States law can be useful to Canadians. There are approximately 20 times more lawyers and law schools in the United States than in Canada and, therefore, there is more U.S. legal information being generated and available. A look at U.S. law can often be helpful to Canadians, particularly in matters involving commercial or business transactions. As we discussed in chapter 9, U.S. decisions can be very instructive in demonstrating how our laws are likely to develop. In instances where Canadian courts or legislature have not dealt with a particular issue, U.S. case law and statutes can be useful. Remember the Internet is a relatively new medium and the body of legal decisions regarding the Internet is very small. It may be necessary and wise to obtain an opinion from a lawyer as to how the Canadian courts are likely to deal with a legal situation involving the Internet.

Here are some resources:

(a) For the latest on U.S. information law, try the site: www.FloridaLawFirm.com/infolaw.html. This is a well-structured site organized under the headings people, places, and things. The site contains a number of original documents, articles, and summaries of U.S. cases and statutes.

(b) There is a site devoted to socially challenged and technologically gifted persons called, you guessed it, Nerd World. This site contains a great deal of information of interest to nerds in general categories ranging from leisure to business. Links to legal-related issues contain a number of articles dealing with Internet- and information-law related subjects. Check out Nerd World at: www.Nerdworld.com.

(c) The New York Law Publishing Company has its own Web page called The Law Journal Extra! located at: www.Ljx.com. This is an excellent all-encompassing U.S. Web page which contains information on news, U.S. law firms, and other U.S. legal resources.

(d) David J. Loundy is an Illinois lawyer with a huge presence on the Internet. His Web page is entitled the E-Law Web page and contains a number of original articles and a comprehensive list of U.S. cases dealing with Internet law. The address is: www.leepfrog.com/ELaw/index.html.

4. Information about privacy and the Internet

(a) Electronic Frontier Canada (EFC) is an organization that actively promotes the right of on-line free speech. The organization is a good source of information dealing with privacy issues and the Internet. The EFC home page may be found at: www.efc.ca.

(b) The U.S. equivalent of EFC is the Electronic Frontier Foundation. Many of the law-related sites that you might choose to visit will contain a blue ribbon icon. This is the symbol of the campaign dedicated to the principle of civil liberties (mostly free speech on the Internet) begun by the Electronic Frontier Foundation. The Electronic Frontier Foundation Web page location is: www.eff.org.

(c) The Office of the Privacy Commissioner of Canada investigates individual complaints and monitors compliance with the Federal Privacy Act. You may contact the commissioner directly at the office's Web site at: infoweb.magi.com/~privcan/.

5. Information about intellectual property on the Internet

(a) The Canadian Intellectual Property Office Web site describes its function as being "responsible for the administration and processing of the greater part of intellectual property in Canada." The Canadian Intellectual Property Office's (CIPO) jurisdiction extends to responsibility for the registration of patents, trademarks, copyrights, and industrial designs. The CIPO Web page address is: patents1.ic.gc.ca.

(b) Philip B. Kerr is an intellectual property lawyer who practises law in Ottawa. His Web page can be found at: www.trytel.com/~pbkerr/index.html. A visitor to Kerr's site will be rewarded with access to a number of interesting and easy-to-read articles on intellectual property issues such as patents, trademarks, and copyright.

(c) For more information about how to register a domain name and for a copy of InterNIC's Rules and Policies, see www.domainregistry.com.

6. **Precedent computer law agreements and forms on the Internet**

(a) The Bitlaw Web page prepared by Daniel A. Tysver, a U.S. attorney, allows you to access sample confidentiality and non-disclosure agreements, employment agreements, Internet policies, and software and Web site development agreements. These agreements can be viewed at no charge. This Web site is located at: www.bitlaw.com.

(b) If you want general information about the law or up-to-date information about prominent trials, check out the Court TV Web page. The Courtroom Television Network is a U.S. broadcasting company that carries a weekly television show on law-related issues. The Web page contains information about cases, statutes, and news. The Internet site of Court TV at www.courttv.com allows visitors to access all types of information including legal forms.

(c) The 'Lectric Law Library is billed as the Net's finest legal resource for legal pros and lay people alike. Of particular interest are sample agreements which can be found at this Web site. The site is located at: www.lectlaw.com.

7. Law firms

There are now hundreds of law firms on the World Wide Web. You are probably best advised to use a law firm in your locality because laws do change depending on whether the subject is governed by provincial or federal laws. A good starting point is the legal e-mail address directory prepared by Carswell Professional Publishing (a legal publisher) at: www.Carswell.com. This site will also provide you with e-mail addresses of accounting, business, and tax professionals.

Smith Lyons is a large Toronto law firm. Its information technology law page is both comprehensive and accessible, and contains more than enough information and articles on computer law for the average person. The page can be found at: www.smithlyons.ca/it/.

A number of Canadian lawyers maintain attractive and well-organized Web sites containing more than just commercial information. Here are some addresses worth checking out:

- Judith Bowers' law list located at:
  www.geocities.com/~jab/law/bowers.html

- Bill Henderson's law library: www.bloorstreet.com

- Peter Sim's Web page: www.mbnet.mb.ca/~psim

- Alan Gahtan's Web site is an excellent starting point for doing legal research. This computer and information technology lawyer's home page allows access to information about Canadian lawyers and law firms on the Internet and, most importantly, allows you to obtain a great deal of information in the form of original articles through his cyberlaw encyclopedia. The address is: www.gahtan.com/alan.

8. **Miscellaneous Web sites**

• Industry Canada maintains one of the largest Web
  sites in Canada. The Industry Canada Web site contains a wealth of information for businesspeople
  ranging from surveys, business statistics, and a list of
  all federally incorporated companies. This site is a
  must for your personal bookmarks and it is located
  at: strategis.ic.gc.ca.

• *Netwatchers* is a monthly on-line magazine dealing
  with cyberspace legal issues and events. It is located
  at: www.emitech.com/netwatchers/front.html.

• Jeff Kuester is a U.S. lawyer who maintains one of the
  best all-encompassing sources of legal information
  on the World Wide Web. His page may be found at:
  www.kuesterlaw.com.

• Quicklaw is the major Canadian legal database operator. For a fee, Quicklaw offers access to over 1 000
  databases and bulletin boards which offer full text
  reports of the latest decisions. The cost of Quicklaw
  service, however, will likely be prohibitive unless
  you are practising law. You may wish to visit the
  Quicklaw home page at: www.qlsys.ca.

• Internet Lawyer is a page maintained by Carey Linde,
  a Vancouver lawyer. The page contains a great deal
  of information organized in an easy-to-use format. If
  you want to access more than just dry legal stuff, have
  a look at Linde's page located at www.netlegal.com.
  You might want to check out the links to "cool sites
  for lawyers" and humour. Check out the personal-
  ized Shakespearian insult service site and the John
  Gotti tribute page.

- FindLaw is a searchable site maintained by the authors of the Webcrawler search engine. The site allows virtually unlimited access to information concerning primarily U.S. legal subjects. It is located at: www.findlaw.com.

- The Hieros Gamos site (www.hg.org/topre search. html) is lacking in actual legal information but will help you locate such information. It has a search system that permits you to access legal libraries to find material. As a bonus, this site also has language dictionaries that will allow you to translate material from English to almost any other language.

- The Virtual Canadian Law Library is a site maintained by the University of Montreal. The site allows you to access a lot of information about legislation, judicial decisions, and Canadian law firms. Have a look at this site at: www.droit.umontreal.ca/doc/biblio/en/index.html.

- The Nanyang Technological University Library in Singapore operates an excellent site for information on law-related topics at: www.Ntu.Ac.Sg/library.

A number of the Canadian law schools now have their own Web pages. Check out the following:

- Osgoode Hall Law School: www.yorku.ca/faculty/osgoode.

- University of Montreal: www.droit.umontreal.ca.

b. MAILING LISTS

When you subscribe to a mailing list, you receive copies of all the e-mail that other members send to the list. If you do not like the mail you receive, you can unsubscribe from the list. Likewise, when you send mail to the list, everyone who is a member gets a copy of your article.

Mailing lists generally fall into two categories. The first is a moderated mailing list in which all messages are reviewed by someone, usually the mailing list administrator, to make sure that the content of the message is on topic before it is distributed to the whole group.

The second type are unmoderated mailing lists in which anything goes. Any notices that you post will be distributed to the mailing list members. Unfortunately, unmoderated discussions can deteriorate into trivial discussions about unrelated topics.

NET NOISE

The garbage that is posted to many unmoderated lists is referred to on the Net as noise.

To join a mailing list you must send a request to the list administrator saying that you want to join. There are a number of popular mailing list management software programs, the most popular being Listserv. As well, any general resource book on the Internet will provide you with detailed commands for finding out about mailing lists, subscribing to them and, if necessary, unsubscribing. It is a good idea to find out about a given mailing list before joining and providing your own views and opinions.

FREQUENTLY ASKED QUESTIONS

Most mailing lists have a file known as a frequently asked questions file — FAQ. The FAQ file will tell you a little bit more about the list and how it operates. Have a look at

the FAQ file before asking a question that hundreds of
other users may have already asked.

Here are some resources you might want to check out:

- Law links - Legal Listservs. This is a World Wide Web
  site maintained by the librarian at the University of
  Chicago. It is an excellent and comprehensive site
  listing of both Canadian and U.S. law–related mailing lists and newsgroups. This site can be found at:
  www.lib.uchicago.nu/llou/lawlist/info.html.

- Call-L. This is a moderated list dealing with issues of
  importance to Canadian law librarians and legal re-
  searchers. Anyone can subscribe to the list. The address is: listserv://listserv@unb.ca.

- EFC-Talk. This list is administered by Electronic
  Frontier Canada (see discussion on privacy and the
  Internet under section **a.** above). The discussion relates to the Charter of Rights and Freedoms and its
  application to the Internet. It is located at: listserv@
  morgan.ucs.mm.ca.

For information on the issue of intellectual freedom and
censorship, you may also want to check out:

- List Serve://listserve@snoopy.ucis.dal.ca.

- Net-lawyers-L. This is a U.S.–based, moderated list
  dealing with Internet legal developments. This is a
  very large list so you should expect a lot of mail. The
  address is: Listserv://listproc@lawlib. wacc.edu.

You may also find a mailing list that appeals to you by
visiting the Indiana University mailing list archives. It is a
database of approximately 13 000 lists that can be searched
by key words. Visit their World Wide Web site at: www.ucs
.indiana.edu/mlarchive.

The Law Guy is a moderated bulletin board service. The Web page is well worth a visit: www.vaxxine.com/mckeown/ law_guy_bbs.html. The Web page contains information on how to sign on as a guest on this BBS. One of the features of The Law Guy is a customized message area enabling a registered user to ask a legal question to the system operator who is a lawyer.

Eric Heels' legal list is a very comprehensive list of law-related mailing lists. You may also wish to visit his Web site which contains a huge collection of articles and other links to law sites. The address is: www.law.cam.ac.uk./guides/ heelsfor.htm.

c. NEWSGROUPS AND DISCUSSION GROUPS

Newsgroups are forums where people with a common interest can exchange information, discuss topics, and ask each other questions. A newsgroup is actually a collection of messages that focuses on a particular subject area. The messages that users write and submit to the newsgroup are known as articles. Sending an article to the newsgroup is referred to as posting an article.

Newsgroups are different than mailing lists. With a mailing list, you receive information via your e-mail program. If you don't like the information you receive, you must delete it. With a newsgroup, you use software called a newsreader. When you review information that has been posted you can pick and choose what you want. Newsgroups allow you to become more selective about what you read. The downside is, however, that the tone of newsgroup postings can be more frivolous because users are not sending their messages to anyone in particular.

Newsgroups are usually distributed over a computer network collectively called UseNet, short for Users Network. There are other news networks but UseNet is easily the largest. If you have an Internet account with a service provider, you will be able to access a newsgroup.

UseNet groups are broken down into hierarchies. Each hierarchy level is separated by a period. For example, "misc.immigration" tells you that the newsgroup discusses miscellaneous issues concerning immigration. Misc.immigration.canada tells you that the discussion will centre around immigration in Canada. The hierarchy, then, allows a user to narrow the search for a newsgroup of interest to him or her.

There are scores of new newsgroups being created every week. If you look at some of the Web sites discussed earlier in this chapter, inevitably you will be directed to newsgroups that may be of interest to you.

NEWSGROUP ETIQUETTE

Although newsgroups can be powerful communication tools, the usefulness of a newsgroup depends on the willingness of the users to follow certain basic rules of cooperation and courtesy:

- Read the newsgroup's FAQ file before posting questions.

- Take a look around first before jumping in. Participants in a newsgroup have a certain way of interacting amongst themselves. They fall into certain styles simply because they have been part of the newsgroup for a period. To communicate effectively with these people, you need to learn the nuances of working with others in a newsgroup.

- Use e-mail if you can. You can imagine the clutter that 100 responses to your article will create when it is posted to the newsgroup. If your article is not going to be of general use to the entire group, ask for private responses by way of e-mail. Conversely, if you want to send a personal reply to a posted question, do so by e-mail.

- Read other replies before sending your own. Be aware that there are a lot of other participants probably thinking the same thing you are. You will not be contributing to the conversation if you say the same thing as someone else.

- Keep it simple. The downside of newsgroup participation is that it can be overwhelming. Imagine being part of ten separate newsgroups and having to read the questions and responses generated by each group. Your peers will appreciate it if your postings and responses are short and to the point.

TIPS AND TRAPS

WHO NEEDS A COMPUTER OR HIGH-TECHNOLOGY LAWYER?

For many people, the need for a computer or high-technology lawyer will be abundantly obvious. For example, it would be foolish to undertake a major system acquisition or to outsource the information-processing department of your company without first obtaining legal advice. For others, the need for a lawyer is less obvious. If you decide to publish a Web page for your consulting business, a computer lawyer is probably not necessary. But if you wish to hire someone to develop a program for you or your company, sell on-line services, or license a program you have developed, you should talk to a computer lawyer.

Consider the following scenario: You spend a great deal of time and effort developing a computer program. Countless hours have been spent coding and debugging, and now the finished product stands a good chance of making a lot of money. Should you be talking to a computer lawyer? Absolutely. What happens if one of your best test versions falls into the wrong hands? What happens if, inadvertently, your licence agreement contains a loop hole that allows any user of your program to distribute copies of it? The end result is obvious: you could end up with nothing for all your hard work and effort.

Or, take the situation where you have quit your job and negotiated a considerable line of credit to start a new business such as an on-line research company. The $1 500 that you spend for some basic legal advice on setting up your business, keeping proper records, and avoiding liability for copyright infringement will likely be well worth the cost in avoiding problems down the road.

In general, if you are unsure whether an issue is legal in the first place, get legal advice. If you are unsure about whether your on-line sales campaign is likely to be considered a pyramid scheme, and therefore illegal, get some legal advice first.

As well, if the contract or transaction involves dealings on an international scale, it is probably a good idea to get legal advice on whether or not laws outside of Canada will apply to the transaction.

If there is any likelihood that a mistake on your part could have catastrophic consequences, get legal advice. For example, your commercial contract with a large financial institution provides that your company will have access to crucial and confidential information. You will want to get some legal advice on ensuring the confidentiality of that information and protecting your company with a well-written contract.

FINDING A LAWYER

You must be comfortable with your lawyer. Choosing a lawyer from the telephone book, especially when you have a specific computer-related issue to be dealt with, is the wrong approach. You will likely need a lawyer with specialized skills and experience. If you approach a lawyer with your specialized problem, he or she should be able to refer you to someone else who fits your needs if he or she is not qualified to help you.

1.   Each province has a law society, incorporated by the provincial legislature, whose responsibility is to set

standards for lawyers. All lawyers must join the law society in the province in which they wish to practise law. The provincial law societies will provide you with a list of lawyers in your area with the expertise you require. For example, the Law Society of Upper Canada in Ontario manages a lawyer referral service. Many law societies also manage toll-free advice lines and sponsor programs where an initial half hour of advice from a lawyer is paid through the law society.

2. Often the best source of finding a good lawyer is through a referral from a friend or a family member. The odds are that if someone you trust has had good dealings with a lawyer, you will too.

3. There are a number of specialized organizations and associations for computer lawyers. If you are unable to find someone who specializes in this area of the law, you might try contacting one of the following groups:

    (a) Computer Law Association at: cla.org

    (b) Canadian Information Technology Law Association. The Web page can be found at: www.it-can.ca

4. Finally, you can always search the Internet for a lawyer. All serious high-technology lawyers will have a home page on the World Wide Web. Some even offer package deal pricing. A lawyer is unlikely to be able to give a firm quotation for a complicated legal transaction such as drafting a lengthy customized electronic data interchange agreement. However, if you intend to use some unique graphic or symbol for your Web page, you should be able to get a firm price quotation from the lawyer to obtain trademark protection for that symbol.

GLOSSARY

Address

The code by which you are identified to all the computers on the Internet. E-mail is delivered to your address. Most addresses follow the format: username@hostname (e.g., jsmith@computer.com).

Bounce

The return of a piece of e-mail because of an error in its delivery.

Browser

A software program that is used to search for information on the World Wide Web.

Brute force attack

A brute force attack is a means of deciphering encrypted information by trying all possible keys until one decrypts the ciphertext. This means of breaking a cipher is usually only possible with the use of a sophisticated computer and an abundance of computing power.

Bulletin Board Service (BBS)

A service that enables users to enter information so that others can read and share that information.

.com

When the letters *.com* appear in an Internet address, they indicate that the host computer is run by a corporation (versus an educational facility (.edu) or other organization (.org)).

Cryptanalysis

Cryptanalysis is the art and science of defeating encrypted communications.

Cryptography

Cryptography is the art and science of keeping communications secure.

Cyberspace

The virtual universe of computer programs and data.

Cybersquatting

The practice of registering one or more domain names for the purpose of later selling the right to use such domain name(s) to persons having a legitimate interest in the use of the name(s).

Defamation

Defamation is any communication that is false and injurious to the reputation of another. Defamation can take two forms: libel is a defamatory statement made in writing; and slander is a defamatory statement made orally.

Domain name

A unique name that identifies your site on the World Wide Web.

Downloading

The electronic transfer of information from one computer to another.

Electronic mail (e-mail)

Electronic mail is a message sent from one person to another in cyberspace via the computer.

Electronic mail policy

A policy statement issued by an employer to its employees outlining the business purposes of the company's e-mail system, the scope of the employer's right to monitor e-mail communications, and guidelines for proper usage. E-mail policies are an effective means of reducing an employer's potential liability stemming from employee initiated lawsuits and third party initiated lawsuits based on an employee's copyright infringement, defamation, and other claims that may arise through an employee's use of e-mail in the workplace. E-mail policies adopted by schools and universities are commonly referred to as Acceptable Use Policies (AUPs).

Encryption

Encryption refers to the process of disguising a legible communication into an unintelligible jumble of characters which can only be unscrambled by the software that performed the encryption.

File transfer protocol (FTP)

An Internet application that allows you to transfer files from a remote computer to your personal computer.

Firewall

A system that lets only certain kinds of messages into a computer network and filters out garbage such as viruses.

Flame

An opinion or criticism strongly expressed in an electronic mail message.

Frequently asked questions (FAQ)

A list of commonly asked questions and answers that is provided to new users of a bulletin board service.

Home page

The initial entry point to a Web document. The home page often acts as a base or main menu which allows or directs access to more detailed information.

Hotlist

A person's selection of his to her favourite Web pages.

Hypertext

Data in a document that is organized to provide links between words or phrases so that related concepts or issues can be linked together. This is the main method by which documents are linked together on the Internet.

Hypertext Markup Language (HTML)

The text format of documents on the World Wide Web. HTML is the language that is used to set up and construct documents, allowing an author to control the design of his or her Web pages by allowing him or her to define elements such as headers, paragraph boundaries, and text formatting.

Listserv

A program that acts as a message switch for e-mail specific subjects. You can subscribe to a list that is a topic of interest to you on a listserv and you will receive all messages that are sent to the list. If you reply to those messages, all other subscribers will see your reply as well.

Mailing list

A list of e-mail addresses used to forward messages (usually related to a specific topic such as law) to groups of people.

Some mailing lists are moderated by persons who decide whether or not to send messages to the entire group.

Netiquette

A play on the word *etiquette* that refers to the proper and tasteful conduct of users on the Internet.

Smart card

A smart card is a plastic laminated card, similar in appearance to a credit card, that contains a computer chip. Smart cards can be used to generate and/or store passwords and encryption keys.

Snail mail

This is a commonly used term used to describe the "old fashioned" mode of postal traffic — sending something by Canada Post. Believe it or not, an actual stamp is required.

Spamming

Spamming is the indiscriminate mass distribution of e-mail messages usually with a commercial intent. Spammers most often distribute their messages by using a mailing list and a computer program that will permit the simultaneous transmission of messages to hundreds or perhaps thousands of Internet users.

Statute of Frauds

The term, Statute of Frauds, is a common designation for statutes that have been adopted by all of the common law provinces and most of the U.S. states. These statutes provide that certain classes of contracts cannot be enforced by a court unless they are documented in writing and signed by the party against whom the contract is sought to be enforced.

System security

This term refers to the measures that a company takes to protect its computer system (and the records and other information it may contain) from attack or destruction from the outside. Such outside threats include hackers, viruses, and destructive natural events such as power outages or fire. System security measures can also be directed toward inside threats such as disgruntled, dishonest, or even nosey employees.

Trademark

A trademark is any word, name, or symbol or any combination thereof adopted and used by a business to distinguish its goods or services from others in the marketplace.

Trade secret

Any formula, pattern, device, or information that is used by a business which remains unknown to the competitors of the business.

Virus

A program that maliciously replicates itself within a computer system or network, destroying data and information in the process.

World Wide Web (WWW or Web)

An information distribution system in which users may create, edit, or browse documents created using HTML.

OTHER TITLES AVAILABLE FROM
SELF-COUNSEL PRESS

STANDARD LEGAL FORMS AND AGREEMENTS

Stephen Sanderson, editor
$16.95

If you don't want the expense of individually designed and printed business or legal forms, but you do want standardized forms to enhance your image and help your business run more smoothly, then you need this book. In all, there are 95 forms covering everything you need in one convenient package.

Includes forms for:

- Letter styles and memo setup
- Partnership Agreement
- Engaging someone's services
- Hiring and dismissal
- Accepting, rejecting, and returning goods
- Collections
- Leasing

CANADIAN LEGAL GUIDE FOR SMALL BUSINESS

Nishan Swais, LL.B.
$21.95

As every owner of a small- to medium-sized business knows, legal questions frequently arise relating to the operation of a business. Yet, it is not always practical to seek the advice of a lawyer for each and every legal matter. This book was written to answer the general question, "What do I, as a business owner, need to know about the law in Canada?"

Written in straightforward language by a lawyer who specializes in business law, the book covers:

- Business structure and company law
- Contract and consumer law
- Dispute resolution
- Legislation affecting businesses
- Commonly used business documents

ORDER FORM

All prices are subject to change without notice. Books are available in book, department, and stationery stores. If you cannot buy the book through a store, please use this order form.
(Please print)

Name _____

Address _____

_____

Charge to: ❑ Visa   ❑ MasterCard

Account Number _____

Expiry Date _____

Signature _____

Shipping and handling will apply.
7% GST will be added.

YES, please send me:

_____ *Standard Legal Guide for Small Business*
_____ *Canadian Legal Guide*

❑ Check here for a free catalogue.

Please send your order to the nearest location:

Self-Counsel Press
1481 Charlotte Road
North Vancouver, BC V7J 1H1

Self-Counsel Press
4 Bram Court
Brampton, ON L6W 3R6

Visit our Web site at: *www.self-counsel.com*